Praise for the Innovative Leadership

A practical guide using comprehensive assessments and practices that develop a balanced Integral leadership approach critical for these fast ever-changing times.

Jim Grote, Founder, Donatos and the Grote Companies

■■■■■■

This Fieldbook takes an insightful journey through the five stages of innovative leadership development—with a fresh perspective. Leaders will find a comprehensive set of tools to help them both personally develop and also to coach their employees. The insight has helped me dramatically improve productivity and effectiveness among the leaders working for me.

Andrew Manzer, President and CEO at Schuyler Hospital

■■■■■■

The Innovative Leadership Fieldbook offers a fresh perspective and thoughtful approach on leadership that helps leaders align their actions with the organizational culture and systems. This alignment is critical in successfully transforming organizations and implementing sustainable change in a complex environment.

Michael Bill, Executive Director Innovation Initiative
Fisher College of Business, The Ohio State University

■■■■■■

As the Innovative Leadership Fieldbook so artfully points out, 'true leaders are both born and made—our leadership skills evolve as we grow'. Had I had insights from this book earlier in my career, including my first CEO role, my leadership development would have been significantly accelerated, helping me better navigate new challenges. Nevertheless, I'm happy to have it now!

Mike Sayre, President and COO at 2Checkout.com

The Innovative Leadership Fieldbook is the perfect blend of important information and personal exploration. Several times, I put the book aside to take stock of who I am today and who I want to be tomorrow. As a leader or leadership coach, The Innovative Leadership Fieldbook is a "must have" for your personal development and your clients. Beautifully written, academically brilliant, and masterfully designed; The Innovative Leadership Fieldbook leads readers on a path to become a better leader and a happier person.

Mike Morrow-Fox, MBA, Vice President of Human Resources and Talent Development, American Heart Association, Great Rivers Affiliate

■■■■■■

The Innovative Leadership Fieldbook offers important insight and gives needed information that would be of great help to leaders of every discipline. It offers a comprehensive set of tools and extensive case studies and examples from real executives that have applied this program with success. The combination of theory and application make this a must read leadership book.

Kamal Aboshamaa, Vice President, R&D, Bolthouse Farms

■■■■■■

The Innovative Leadership Fieldbook tackles the complex topic of leadership and makes it real, practical, and powerful for leaders in all walks of life. I have used elements of this approach in an organizational transformation and found it delivered significant positive results. This book explains the key domains of leadership required for complex change and how to build them in yourself and your team.

Rob Richardson – CIO Large Global Manufacturing Firm

INNOVATIVE LEADERSHIP FIELDBOOK

Field-Tested Integral Approaches to Developing Leaders, Transforming Organizations and Creating Sustainability

BY MAUREEN METCALF MARK PALMER

First Published by
Integral Publishers
1418 N. Jefferson Ave.
Tucson, AZ 85712

Published in the United States with printing and
distribution in the United Kingdom, Australia,
and the European Union.

© 2011 Integral Publishers

*"Define Personal Vision and Checklist of Values" from
Peter Senge, Charlotte Roberts, Richard Ross, Bryan
Smith and Art Kleiner, Fifth Discipline Fieldbook,
New York: Doubleday, 1994, used with permission.*

ISBN: 978-1-4507-9176-2

First Printing September 2011

Cover Design, Graphics and Layout by
Creative Spot - www.creativespot.com

Acknowledgments

Contributing Authors: Belinda Gore and Dena Paluck

The theoretical giants on whose hard work we built our structure: Terry O'Fallon, Susann Cook-Greuter, Ken Wilber, Belinda Gore, Cindy Wigglesworth, Hilke Richmer, Roxanne Howe-Murphy, and Peter Senge, who not only shared their theories but whose ongoing guidance and encouragement helped us create a solid framework that is theoretically grounded and comprehensive.

Our friends and colleagues who served as constant cheerleaders, listened to the stories and dreams about the book, and helped us make it come to fruition.

Our clients who participated as case studies, as well as MBA students who gave feedback on the book by virtue of doing the graduate work using this Fieldbook.

Our families who inspired us to be thoughtful and dedicated to our work, and to contribute to the world in a meaningful way.

Our Publisher, Graphic Design and Layout firm, reviewers, editors, endorsers, thought partners including Chad Stewart, and countless others who spent untold hours making this possible.

Table of Contents

PREFACE:
Re-Visioning Leadership and Innovation

You've enhanced your productivity by adopting new technology. You've streamlined your operations and aligned your teams, meticulously implementing the details of your strategic plan. You've fully invested to better innovate the way you run your business. But have you invested in the innovation of your leadership? Are you getting the business results you need to thrive?

Without question, today's organizational challenges have made recurrent innovation a requisite part of your business. As you are well aware, applying innovative strategies can be exhaustive, spanning everything from process and products to marketing, acquisitions and customer experience. Decisions involving innovation will often be among the most influential choices executive teams ultimately make toward a company's future outlook.

Yet despite its broad applicability, most innovation is largely geared toward enhancements in technology, such as developing better goods and services or redesigning system functionality. Though good management teams implicitly understand the importance of boosting system performance, very few of them comprehend the need for innovation within an equally crucial yet often overlooked dimension of their core business: *their leadership.*

More specifically, companies often seriously neglect the ways in which their leaders actually relate with the organization, envision strategy, and most fundamentally, steward their own personal and professional growth. The way you, as a leader, perceive your business is itself an untapped opportunity for innovation. Streamlining the way your business works is essential, but merely innovating the functionality of your systems can only address half your issues. Even worse, it can blind your strategic vision concerning performance improvement and operational excellence.

How did such a broad notion as innovation get reduced to technological advancement and piecemeal strategies that focus solely on improving functional systems?

An Ever-Changing Organizational Climate

Simply consider today's vast operating complexities, as well as their egregious by-products stemming from twenty years of accelerated globalization, market volatility and advanced commoditization. Escalating uncertainty and resulting economic decline have become staggeringly familiar. Companies struggle to match their past performances with considerably fewer resources. Entire segments, and in some cases entire industries, once thriving a mere decade ago, are now experiencing immense decline.

In short, the current state of organizational climates is wildly ambivalent. The assertion of unlimited growth and wealth appears unlikely, at best. Resembling Darwin's "survival of the fittest," market forces pressured the fate of organizations, generously rewarding executive teams that adapted while dispassionately retiring the less successful. Even in cases where business innovations enhance the bottom-line, success is often a short-term outlook.

But here's the glaring irony of the situation: the accelerated growth of technological innovation eventually created an increased need for it; never mind that most of those emerging innovations were largely experimental to begin with. The near exponential drive of tech innovation, fueled largely by a need for competitive relevance, contributed to conditions that produced hostile operating environments. Interestingly, it wasn't a lack of innovation that fed instability across markets, since the need for it took on increased urgency. Though technology innovations, at least in theory, largely improved business efficiency, they also compounded competitive pressures, which accelerated production and increased services, which further decreased business-time horizons, and so on. In summary, continual advancements in systems efficiency, driven by evolving technologies, developed at an unprecedented rate and caused accelerating disruptions in every sector.

The ensuing fallout has proved deeply problematic. Innovating functional efficiency has become the sole focus of strategy at the expense of leadership vision and cultural cohesion. This has created significant dissonance between an organization's purpose and day-to-day functioning. Companies focused their energies and resources on performance training, yet failed to foster sophisticated thinking, interaction, and comprehensive decision-making among their leaders. This has fed a common yet unsophisticated assumption that technical competency was somehow equivalent to strategic vision.

The challenge of exploring and applying innovation is also a challenge to deepen your leadership. Your perspective as a leader, along with the cultural alignment of your team and organization, must keep pace with functional enhancements. Accelerated developments in technology extended through increased globalization created unexpected anomalies in market forces, leading to innovative solutions that were geared primarily toward streamlining systems. Unbridled growth in systems technology spawned one-sided innovation, all the while crippling advancements in strategic vision and cultural cohesion.

In essence then, conventional innovation has been reduced to merely improving an organization's functional processes. This one-sided version of innovation not only drove market volatility, it also marginalized new organizational strategies, particularly those emerging to navigate a recently flattened global economy. Companies were applying technology innovation to resolve issues that were created by primarily focusing on technological systems in the first place. In fact, entering the 21st century, nearly two-thirds of Total Quality Management (TQM) programs reportedly failed along with 70% of the reengineering initiatives aimed at fostering organizational stability (Senge, 1999, pp. 5-6). Leaders of the corporate reengineering movement report that the success rate for reengineer efforts for Fortune 1000 companies is below 50%, and possibly only 20% (Strebel, 2000, p. 86). Companies clearly needed innovation to traverse the new economic landscape, yet experienced little success since the solutions they sought were incomplete to begin with.

Based on these failures, today's organizational complexity requires you to seriously consider more comprehensive approaches to innovation and leadership. At some point, exclusively focusing on performance analytics concerning systems can prove costly. The opportunity to enhance your innovative capacity must extend beyond increasing functionality, which is crucial but incomplete when implemented alone. If, in addition to developing better functional processes, you begin to also clarify your vision, growing your leadership capacity, and building a cohesive company culture—you will achieve much greater and more sustainable success.

The Opportunity of Innovative Leadership

As we've discussed, the overwhelming focus of today's organizational solutions are almost entirely oriented toward system functionality. This is foundationally necessary, but only part of your total picture. Being guided by more strategically inclusive decisions may be the difference between managing failure and creating tangible success. Your leadership must be supported by more balanced innovation, comprehensively aligning your vision, teams and systems by integrating enhanced leadership perspective with system efficiency.

This balanced approach to leadership and innovation is transformative, for both you and your organization, and can help you to respond more effectively to challenges exerted within and outside the enterprise. Innovative Leadership affords you the means to successfully adapt in ways that allow optimal performance, even within an organizational climate fraught with continual change and complexity. Conceptually, it synthesizes models from developmental, communications and systems theory, delivering better insight than singular approaches. Innovative Leadership gives you the capacity to openly recognize and critically examine aspects of yourself, as well as your organization's culture and systems in the midst of any circumstance.

Defining an Innovative Leader

What are specific qualities that differentiate an innovative leader from a traditional leader? In our time of rapid business, social and ecological change, a successful leader is a leader who can continually:

- Clarify and effectively articulate vision
- Link that vision to attainable strategic initiatives
- Develop themselves and influence the development of other leaders
- Build effective teams by helping colleagues enact their own leadership strengths
- Cultivate alliances and partnerships
- Anticipate and respond to both challenges and opportunities aggressively
- Develop robust and resilient solutions
- Develop and test hypothesis like a scientist. Scientifically develop and test hypothesis
- Measure, learn and refine on an ongoing basis

To further illustrate some of the qualities of innovative leadership, we offer this comparison between traditional leadership and innovative leadership:

TRADITIONAL LEADERSHIP	INNOVATIVE LEADERSHIP
Leader is guided primarily by desire for personal success and peripherally by organizational success	Leader is humbly guided by a more altruistic vision of success based on both performance and the value of the company's positive impact
Leadership decision style "monarchical;" leader has all the answers	Leader leverages team for answers as an adjunct to decision-making process
Leader picks a course in "black/white" manner; tends to dogmatically stay the course	Leader perceives and behaves like a scientist: continually measuring and testing for improvement
Leader focuses on being technically correct and in charge	Leader is continually learning and developing self and others
Leader tends to the numbers and primarily quantitative measures that drive those numbers	Leader tends to financial performance, customer satisfaction, employee engagement, community impact, and cultural cohesion

We invite you to explore this fieldbook as a way to innovate your leadership in a climate of vexing uncertainty and partial solutions. We introduce you to unique tools designed to help leaders and their organizations tackle unprecedented complexity. Drawing from numerous case studies and recorded interaction among executives, managers, and consultants, this volume is the summation of cutting edge insights and methods aimed at improving personal and professional development.

INTRODUCTION:
Innovative Leadership

Leadership and innovation are two of the most compelling topics in Organizational Development. Even so, and despite the volume of resources exploring both topics, most approaches provide directional solutions that are merely anecdotal. We know that leadership plays a critical role in a company's long-term success, and that innovation has become a strategic necessity in today's business environment. Both leadership and innovation are perhaps more impactful today than ever before. Technology and increased access to information continue to accentuate their roles, yet companies are often too overrun with change to handle the throng of emerging demands.

Still, ensuing questions on how to lead and where to innovate remain puzzlingly philosophical: What is the role of leadership in a time of looming uncertainty? How will companies innovate to overcome challenges that are largely unprecedented? In a new climate of business, what is the formula for creating success in both areas?

This fieldbook is designed precisely to help answer those questions and perform a critical self-evaluation. Though its premise is fundamentally about leadership, it is equally an account of innovation. Leadership needs innovation the way innovation demands leadership, and by marrying them we can improve our capacity for growth.

This book explores a number of approaches to elaborate on both fields, not just conceptually, but tangibly by providing exercises designed to enhance your leadership skills. Most importantly, any meaningful advancement concerning both must originate from the leader. In other words, becoming a better leader and optimizing innovation jointly hinge on the leader authentically examining his or her inner makeup.

Even so, you must diligently address some challenging limitations. Despite their collective importance, conventional applications of leadership and innovation have often proved elusive and even problematic in real-world scenarios. For example: if the leadership team of a struggling organization drives initiatives that focus solely on making innovative changes to incentives, products and services, without also advancing strategic purpose and team solidarity, they will still miss the greater potential to create a meaningful turn-around in company culture. Productivity and system improvements are undoubtedly critical, but how employees make sense of their work experience is equally vital. Implementing products and functionality at the expense of also creating a better team environment or a more supportive company culture often appears as lopsided decision-making and shortsighted leadership.

Knowing that the future of organizations is irreversibly tied to a world of erratic change, we can no longer afford to improve our systems and offerings without equally advancing our capacity for leadership. Empathy and the ability to inspire cultural alignment offer your organization significant merit, and must be implemented as shrewdly as strategic planning.

Combining leadership with innovation, then, requires you to transform the way you perceive yourself, others, and your business. By vigorously looking into your own experience, including motivations, inclinations, interpersonal skills and proficiencies, you can optimize your effectiveness in ways that deeply resonate with the realities around you. Through deep examination and reflective engagement, you learn to balance the hard skills you have acquired with meaningful introspection, all the while setting the stage for further growth. In essence, you discover how to strategically and tactically innovate leadership the same way you innovate in other aspects of your business.

Marrying Innovation and Leadership

Let us explore innovative leadership in a more tangible way by defining it in practical terms. This, of course, begs the obvious question: what does innovative leadership really mean?

It is important to first understand each topic beyond its more conventional meaning. For example, most definitions of leadership alone are almost exclusively fashioned around emulating certain kinds of behaviors: leader X did "this" to achieve success, and leader Y did "that" to enhance company performance.

Even if initially useful, such approaches are still essentially formulas for imitating leadership, and are therefore likely ineffectual over the long-term. Innovative leadership cannot be applied as a monolithic theory nor as simple prescriptive guidance. Rather, it must take place through your own native intelligence and stem from your own unique sensibilities.

In order to enhance this unique awareness process you will need a much more foundational basis from which to explore both topics, which means talking about them in a different context entirely.

Let's start by straightforwardly defining leadership:

> **Leadership is a process of influencing people directionally and tactically, affecting change in intentions, actions, culture and systems.**

Within this context and above all else, leadership is influencing: directional influence in the sense that it imparts inspiration toward others; tactical influence in the sense of employing functional execution.

Put differently: leadership influences an individual's intentions and cultures by inspiring purpose and alignment. It equally influences an individual's actions and organized systems by executing tactical decision-making.

Likewise, and as an extension of leadership, innovation refers to the novel ways in which we advance that influence personally, culturally, behaviorally and systematically.

> **Innovation is a novel advancement that shapes organizations: personally, culturally, behaviorally and systematically.**

Notice here that in addition to tying the relationship of leadership to innovation, we're also linking them as an essential part of our individual experience. Like leadership and innovation, the way you experience and influence the world is defined through a mutual interplay of personal, cultural, behavioral and systematic events. These core dimensions which ground leadership and innovation also provide the contextual summation of your total experience on any given occasion.

Optimally then, leadership is influencing through an explicit balancing of those core dimensions. In response, innovation naturally follows as a creative advancement of this basic harmony. Our personal experience, leadership and innovation are all innately connected, and share a deep contextual make-up.

Therefore, marrying leadership with innovation allows you to ground and articulate both in a way that can create a context for dynamic personal development.

An Innovative Leader influences by engaging self, culture and systems equally.

Though we are, in a sense, defining innovative leadership very broadly, we are also making a distinct point. We are saying that, in actuality, the core aspects that comprise your experience, whether personal, cultural, behavioral or systematic, are never mutually exclusive. If you affect one, you affect them all.

Innovative leadership is based on the recognition that those four aspects exist simultaneously in all experiences, and already influence every interactive experience we have. So if, for example, you implement a strategy to re-align a company's value system over the next five years, you will also affect personal motivations, company culture, and behavioral outcomes. Influencing one aspect, in this case, functional systems, affects the other aspects since all four mutually shape that given occasion. To deny the mutual interplay of any one of the four aspects is missing the full picture. You can only build innovative leadership by addressing reality in the most comprehensively available fashion.

Measuring Innovative Leadership

We measure innovative leadership in two very distinct ways; we call these primary qualities **Capacity** and **Competency.**

Capacity describes a leader's ability to take another's point of view, and to communicate, influence, and drive the adoption of leadership principles throughout various levels of organizational culture. In this context, we are deliberately giving special attention to the more subjective qualities of innovative leadership, such as taking other perspectives and aligning organizational values. We are not yet considering aspects that are action or behavior-oriented, which include measures like performance, action or functionality. In essence, capacity describes areas like the development of complex thinking, the ability to take multiple perspectives, empathy engagement, leader type expression and personal resilience.

> **Capacity describes our ability to introspect, reflect and take the perspective of others. It is subjective.**

Competency accounts for a leader's overall proficiency in hard skills, functional expertise, and systems efficiency. In this case, we are exploring innovative leadership as applied to performance, execution and systems. Competency, in this context, is simply proficiency in the business of your organization; it entails all areas of the enterprise that require skills shaped by mostly objective or quantitative measures, such as management acumen and systems execution. Most available resources describing leadership address hard skills. Much of this fieldbook will maintain a more focused discussion on capacity.

> **Competency describes our ability to organize and apply facts, such as tactical skills and functional expertise. It is more objective.**

To summarize: innovative leadership requires a fundamental examination and balancing of your experience along four core aspects: personal, cultural, behavioral, and systematic, that can be gauged as both **capacity** (subjective ability) and **competency** (objective proficiency).

Innovative leadership grows natively from your own realistic self-exploration, allowing you to authentically engage leadership beyond tactical deliberation and systems.

Domains of Innovative Leadership

Figure I-1 Five Domains of Innovative Leadership

Leadership Behaviors

Situational Analysis

Resilience

Developmental Perspective

Leader Type

The first five chapters of this fieldbook explore the five domains of innovative leadership in more depth – reflected in Figure 1-1

What is truly innovative in this fieldbook is the overall comprehensiveness of the model. Theorists have looked at each of these domains separately over many years, and have suggested that mastering one or two of them is typically sufficient for effective leaders. We submit that while that may have been true in a less complex world, it is no longer the case. As the 21st-century unfolds, the most effective leaders will have a much more holistic view than any other time in history. In the following chapters, we will define and describe each individual domain of innovative leadership and how they interact.

After fully defining innovative leadership, we move to Section II: "Building Innovative Leadership Capacity," where we offer a six-step process in a workbook format. It includes tools and practices for each step in the process designed to support you in enhancing your practical effectiveness as an Innovative Leader. The steps in this process are:

- Create a compelling vision of your future
- Analyze your situation and strengths
- Plan your journey
- Build your team and communicate
- Take Action
- Embed innovation systematically

Each step of the process poses questions for reflection. It is the comprehensiveness of this reflection coupled with the exercises that will give you insight into yourself and your organization. This insight is required to change yourself and your organization concurrently or to manage your internal change in the context of an organization that you cannot or do not want to change.

Figure I-2 Leadership Development Process

1. Create a Compelling Vision of Your Future
2. Analyze Your Situation & Strengths
3. Plan Your Journey
4. Build Your Team & Communicate
5. Take Action
6. Embed Innovation Systematically

Learn & Refine

Getting the Most from the Fieldbook

Before you get started, take a moment to think about why you purchased this fieldbook. Setting goals and understanding your intentions and expectations about the exercises will help you focus on identifying and driving your desired results.

In order to help clarify, consider the following questions:

- What are the 5-7 events and/or choices that brought you to where you are professionally and personally?

- How did these events/choices contribute to choosing to buy and use this fieldbook?

- What stands out in the list you have made? Are there any surprises or patterns?

- What do you hope to gain from your investment in leadership development?

- What meaningful impact will it produce in your professional career and personal life?

In addition to your refection on the above questions, here are some ideas we recommend to help you get the most out of this experience. It is our experience that people who adhere to the following agreements tend to have a deeper and more enriching overall experience. By participating in this fashion, you will generate a richer evaluation of yourself and most effectively take advantage of what this fieldbook has to offer.

Take a moment to reflect on the guidelines below:

AGREEMENT	RELATED ACTION OR BEHAVIOR
1. Be fully present	Let go of thoughts about other activities while you read. Bring your full attention to the work.
2. Take responsibility for your own success	Act as though you are 100% responsible for the outcome of your engagement with this material.
3. Participate as fully as possible	Complete all the exercises to the best of your abilities. Apply the concepts and skills that work best for you, and modify those that do not.
4. Practice good life management	Invest time at scheduled intervals to work on the materials when you are at your best mentally and emotionally.
5. Lean into optimal discomfort; take risks without overwhelming yourself.	Be candid, open, and direct. Allow yourself to be curious and vulnerable.
6. Take the process seriously, and more importantly take yourself lightly. Make this positive and rewarding experience.	Allow yourself balance. Find the learning and humor in both your successes and mistakes. Most importantly, have fun!

How to Use the Fieldbook

After this introduction, each subsequent chapter builds to form a complete approach to developing innovative leadership. The first section of the book provides the conceptual framework. The second section guides you through a series of exercises to help ground those ideas in a more practical fashion. We recommend that you use the following sequence to help efficiently process the material:

1. Read Intently

Read the chapter through completely, as we introduce and illustrate an integrated set of concepts for each domain in building innovative leadership.

2. Contemplate

Using a set of carefully chosen applications and specifically designed exercises will help you to embody the work and bring the concepts to life. Through a process of dynamic examination and reflection, you will be encouraged to contemplate some significant, real-life implications of change. Many of the exercises can be done on your own, yet others are designed to be conducted with input from your colleagues such as seeing their perception of your strengths and weaknesses.

3. Link Together Your Experience

As you sequentially build your understanding, you will begin noticing habits and conditioned patterns that can present you clear opportunities for growth. Though you may encounter personal resistance along the way, you will also discover new and exciting strengths. Once you have completed the process, you will have created a plan to grow as an innovative leader. Ultimately, implementing that plan will be up to you and your team.

As you become more adept at using these ideas, you will find yourself increasingly capable of proactive engagement with the concepts along with an ability to respond to situations requiring innovative leadership with greater capacity.

REFLECTIONS

What innovative challenges does your organization face?

How does your organization support effective
leadership for innovation?

In what ways would you consider yourself
an innovative leader?

How do you personally connect with
leadership and innovation?

Where are the opportunities for you
to be an innovative leader?

What would make you and your organization
more effective in leading innovation
beyond products, services and systems?

Leadership Behaviors

Situational Analysis

Resilience

Developmental Perspective

Leader Type

SECTION I

Five Domains of Innovative Leadership

Section 1 - "Five domains of Innovative Leadership" consists of the first five chapters of this Fieldbook and explores the five domains of innovative leadership in more depth. These domains (chapters) are reflected in the graphic above:

Each chapter offers a definition of the key domain; explains the role it plays in innovative leadership; gives an example of the models we use and provides an example or case study to demonstrate how we have applied these domains to improve leadership and organizational performance. These five key domains are interconnected and must be considered as a whole to build truly innovative leadership.

This model serves as the foundation that you will build on in Section II where you will take action to become an innovative leader.

Innovative Leadership Assessment

Leadership Behaviors

Situational Analysis

Resilience

Developmental Perspective

Leader Type

Following is a short self assessment to help you identify your own innovative leadership scores. It is organized by the five domains of innovative leadership and will give you a general sense of where you can focus your efforts to improve your innovative leadership capacity. As you progress through the book, you will find information on the full assessments if you are interested in more in-depth and thorough analysis of your current capacity.

We encourage you to take this assessment as a way to get a snapshot of where you excel and where you may want to focus your developmental activities and energies.

Score Yourself on Awareness of Leader Type and Self Management

Think about your level of response to work situations during the past three months:

Never (1)   Rarely (2)   Sometimes (3)   Often (4)   Almost always (5)

1. I have taken a leadership type assessment such as the Enneagram, Myers Briggs Type Indicator or DISC, and used this information about myself to increase my effectiveness.   **1 2 3 4 5**

2. I use the insight from this assessment to understand my type - specifically I understand my gifts and limitations and try to leverage my strengths and manage my limitations.   **1 2 3 4 5**

3. I have a reflection practice where I understand, actively monitor and work with my "fixations". (a fixation is a negative thought pattern)   **1 2 3 4 5**

4. I have a clear sense of who I am and what I want to contribute in the world.   **1 2 3 4 5**

5. I manage my emotional reactions to allow me to respond with socially appropriate behavior.   **1 2 3 4 5**

6. I am aware of what causes me stress and actively manage it.   **1 2 3 4 5**

7. I have positive coping strategies.   **1 2 3 4 5**

8. I actively seek ways to feel empowered even when the organization may not empower me in a given situation.   **1 2 3 4 5**

Total Score

- ◢ If your overall score in this category is 24 or less, it's time to pay attention to your leadership type and self management.

- ◢ If your overall score is 32 or above, Congratulations! You are self aware and using your leadership type to increase your effectiveness.

Score Yourself on Developmental Perspective Aligned with Innovation

Think about your level of response to work situations during the past three months:

Never (1)   Rarely (2)   Sometimes (3)   Often (4)   Almost always (5)

1. I have a sense of life purpose and do work that is generally aligned with that purpose.   1 2 3 4 5

2. I am motivated by the impact I make on the world more than on personal notoriety.   1 2 3 4 5

3. I try to live my life according to my personal values.   1 2 3 4 5

4. I believe that collaboration across groups and organizations is important to accomplish our goals.   1 2 3 4 5

5. I believe that getting business results must be balanced with treating people fairly and kindly as well as impact on our customers and community.   1 2 3 4 5

6. I seek input from others consistently to test my thinking and expand my perspective.   1 2 3 4 5

7. I think about the impact of my work on the many elements of our community and beyond.   1 2 3 4 5

8. I am open and curious, always trying new things and learning from all of them.   1 2 3 4 5

9. I appreciate the value of rules and am willing to question them in a professional manner in service of meeting our goals and improving the service we provide to our customers.   1 2 3 4 5

Total Score

◢ If your overall score in this category is 27 or less, it's time to pay attention to your developmental level including testing your current level and focusing on developing in this area.

◢ If your score is 36 or above, congratulations! Your developmental level appears to be aligned with innovate leadership yet this assessment is only a subset of a full assessment.

Score Yourself on Resilience

Think about your level of response to work situations during the past three months:

Never (1)   Rarely (2)   Sometimes (3)   Often (4)   Almost always (5)

1. I consistently take care of my physical needs such as getting enough sleep and exercise.   1 2 3 4 5

2. I have a sense of purpose and get to do activities that contribute to that purpose daily.   1 2 3 4 5

3. I have a high degree of self awareness and manage my thoughts actively.   1 2 3 4 5

4. I have a strong support system consisting of a healthy mix of friends, colleagues, and family.   1 2 3 4 5

5. I can reframe challenges to find something of value in most situations.   1 2 3 4 5

6. I build strong trusting relationships at work.   1 2 3 4 5

7. I am aware of my own self talk and actively manage it.   1 2 3 4 5

8. I have a professional development plan that includes gaining skills and additional perspectives.   1 2 3 4 5

Total Score

- ◢ If your overall score in this category is 24 or less, it's time to pay attention to your resilience.

- ◢ If your score is 32 or above, congratulations! You are likely performing well in the area of resilience yet this assessment is only a subset of the full resilience assessment.

Score Yourself on Managing Alignment of Self and Organization

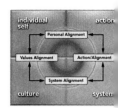

Think about your level of response to work situations during the past three months:

Never (1)   Rarely (2)   Sometimes (3)   Often (4)   Almost always (5)

1. I am aware of my own passions and values .   1 2 3 4 5

2. My behavior reflects my goals and values consistently.   1 2 3 4 5

3. I feel safe pushing back when I am asked to do things that are not aligned   1 2 3 4 5
    with my values.

4. I am aware that my behavior and decisions as a leader have a significant   1 2 3 4 5
    impact on the organization's structure and culture.

5. I am deliberate about aligning the organization's pay and performance   1 2 3 4 5
    systems with the types of behaviors we want to encourage. (both results
    and behaviors)

6. The organization's key measures and systems encourage the right actions   1 2 3 4 5
    aligned with the culture, and discourage actions that will damage the
    organization or make me uncomfortable.

7. I am aware of how my values align with those of the organization and where   1 2 3 4 5
    we are misaligned; I take steps to encourage changes in the culture such as
    talking about our values and reinforcing what we say we care about.

Total Score

➤ If your overall score in this category is 21 or less, it's time to pay attention
   to my alignment with the organization and also the alignment within the
   organization that I am able to impact.

➤ If your score is 28 or above, congratulations! You are well aligned with the
   organization and the organization's culture and systems are well aligned.

Score Yourself on Leadership Behaviors

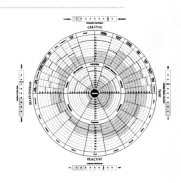

Think about your level of response to work situations during the past three months:

Never (1)   Rarely (2)   Sometimes (3)   Often (4)   Almost always (5)

1. I tend to be proactive – I anticipate what is coming next and actively manage   **1 2 3 4 5**
    it. (depending on role – this may happen primarily in my personal life)

2. I focus on creating results in a way that encourages others to grow and   **1 2 3 4 5**
    develop while accomplishing their tasks.

3. I think about the impact of my actions on the overall organization rather than   **1 2 3 4 5**
    just getting the job done.

4. I see how my work contributes to the overall organizational success and   **1 2 3 4 5**
    deliberately try to improve myself and the organization.

5. I take time to mentor others – even when I am busy.   **1 2 3 4 5**

6. I consider myself a personal learner because of the time I spend reading and   **1 2 3 4 5**
    trying new ideas and activities. I am curious.

7. I have the courage to speak out in a professional manner when asked to do   **1 2 3 4 5**
    something I disagree with.

8. I accomplish results by working with and through others in a positive and   **1 2 3 4 5**
    constructive manner.

Total Score

◢ If your overall score in this category is 24 or less, it's time to pay attention to
your leadership behaviors and look for ways to develop in alignment with
your goals.

◢ If your score is 32 or above, congratulations! You are likely performing well
in the area of leadership behaviors but this assessment is only a subset of a full
leadership behavior assessment.

CHAPTER 1:
Leader Type

Figure 1-1 Five Domains of Innovative Leadership

Leadership Behaviors

Situational Analysis

Resilience

Developmental Perspective

Leader Type

The Importance of Leader Type

Part of the challenge in building innovative leadership is learning to leverage the clarity of your introspection. Looking inside yourself, examining the make-up of your inner being, enables you to function in a highly grounded way, rather than operating from the innate biases of more uninformed decision-making.

First and foremost, when thinking about leadership, start by simply considering your disposition, tendencies, inclinations and ways of being. Innovative leadership hinges on understanding the simple, native manner in which you show up in your life. One way to observe is by examining aspects of your inner being, often called leader type, which reflect the leader's personality type. The Leader Personality Type (referred to going forward as Leader Type) has a critical influence on who you are as a leader. It is an essential foundation of your personal make-up and greatly shapes the effectiveness of your leadership. The ancient adage of "Know Thyself," attributed to various Greek philosophers, holds true as a crucial underpinning in leadership performance.

Your ability to use deep introspection relies on your development of a capacity for self-understanding and self-awareness. Both allow you profound openness of perspective as well as a greater understanding of others. These critical traits support leaders' abilities to self-regulate, communicate effectively with others, and encourage personal learning. You can employ a profound understanding of leader type for both yourself and others as a powerful tool to promote effective leadership.

It is important to keep in mind that this particular notion of type is native to your being and generally does not change significantly over the course of your life. This is an essential point: by ascertaining the distinct "shape" of your type, as well as that of others around you, you can begin to see situations without the bias of your own perceptions. You are then in a better position to leverage what you and others actually demonstrate, rather than acting from naive speculation. You learn to deeply understand the inner movements of your strengths, weaknesses, and core patterns. Typing tools are helpful in promoting this kind of self-knowledge and pattern recognition.

By learning about these patterns, you can gain perspective on your life and start connecting the dots among your different experiences. Most of us have a concept about how we behave, but that idea is likely clouded and not entirely true. One of the hardest things for most people is to see themselves accurately. How astonishing it is to see through the clouds and recognize yourself clearly.

— Deep Living, Roxanne Howe Murphy

Learning at this deeper level--from your personal, inner dynamics and immediate experience--can offer remarkable insight into areas of your character you tend to exaggerate or overemphasize.

Self-awareness and the capacity for self-management are foundational to innovative leadership and overall leadership effectiveness. By becoming aware of your inherent gifts as well as those of others, you are able to improve your personal effectiveness and that of the teams and departments with which you work.

The Enneagram Model and Leader Type

There are several credible typing tools, some of which are used by a wide range of organizations. Prominent examples include: Myers Briggs Type Indicator, DISC, Big Five Personality Test, and the Enneagram. Each of these models has particular strengths in their presentations, as well as certain weaknesses. Their overall purpose is to help you make objective sense of the thought and behavior patterns of yourself and other people.

Self-awareness, the practice of engaging in self-reflection and achieving clarity of insight, being conscious of one's own identity, and the extent to which perceptions about one's self are accurate and compatible with others' observations, play a pivotal role in leadership. Self-aware leaders self-regulate cognitions, emotions, and behavior more effectively depending on the situation, evaluate their impact on others, and possess higher levels of emotional intelligence.

Thus, they become more versatile in their leadership and may perform better. Consequently, successful leader development is foremost personal development. The Enneagram, one of the most comprehensive systems for understanding personality [leader type] and human development, offers considerable merit to support leaders to become more aware of themselves and others.

—Hilke Richmer, Doctoral Dissertation.

As we observed through Hilke Richmer's research project, the Enneagram can be a very powerful typing model. Let's continue to explore the concept of type by also using the Enneagram as our primary tool to assess leader type.

Figure 1-2 Enneagram

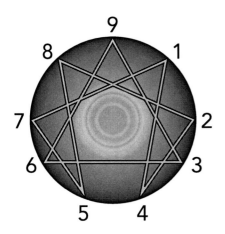

The Enneagram can be a dynamic map of leader type that reveals how you organize experience and find meaning within it. The Enneagram describes nine distinct patterns of attitude and behavior that help to reveal an array of reasons supporting why you think and behave in the ways you do. Using the knowledge of what comprises the Enneagram's nine types can provide you a foundation for better understanding yourself, as well as maintaining healthy relationships through understanding the needs and perspectives of others.

The Enneagram symbol is a circle with nine points, representing the nine types native within all human experience, connected in a distinctive pattern of intersecting lines.

The Enneagram, like other tools, offers you a framework and language to discuss what you perceive about the intentions and see in the behaviors of yourself and others. Each Enneagram type is based on a pattern of what you pay attention to, or more specifically, your naturally occurring perceptions and preferences. By understanding the types of experiences you habitually reinforce and put energy into, you can observe yourself more accurately and develop more self-awareness. By enhancing self-awareness, you can exercise more choice about your own actions rather than engaging in patterns of thought, emotion, and behavior in an automatic, habitual, unconscious fashion. This insight alone will allow you to tailor personal and professional goals to achieve better results.

TABLE 1-1 ENNEAGRAM TYPES

Type 1 — Reformer: The Rational, Idealistic Type

I am a principled, idealistic type. I am conscientious and ethical with a strong sense of right and wrong behavior. I can be a teacher, crusader and advocate for change, always striving to improve things, but sometimes afraid of making mistakes. Well-organized, orderly and fastidious, I try to maintain high standards but can slip into being critical and perfectionistic. I typically have problems with resentment and impatience.

At My Best: I am wise, discerning, realistic and noble. I can be morally heroic.

Type 2 — Helper: The Caring, Interpersonal Type

I am a caring, interpersonal type. I am empathetic, sincere and warm-hearted. I am friendly, generous and self-sacrificing, but can also be sentimental, flattering and people pleasing. I am well-meaning and driven to be close to others, but can slip into doing things for others in order to be needed. I typically have problems with possessiveness and with acknowledging my own needs.

At My Best: I am unselfish and altruistic, and have unconditional love for others.

Type 3 — Achiever: The Success-Oriented, Pragmatic Type

I am an adaptable, success-oriented type. I am self-assured, attractive and charming. Ambitious, competent and energetic, I can also be status-conscious and highly driven for advancement. I am diplomatic and poised, but can also be overly concerned with my image and what others think of me. I typically have problems with over focus on work and competitiveness.

At My Best: I am self-accepting, authentic and a role model who inspires others.

Type 4 — Individualist: The Sensitive, Withdrawn Type

I am an introspective, romantic type. I am self-aware, sensitive and reserved. I am emotionally honest, creative and personal, but can also be moody and self-conscious. Withholding myself from others due to feeling vulnerable, I can also feel scornful and exempt from ordinary ways of living. I typically have problems with melancholy, self-indulgence and self-pity.

At My Best: I am inspired and highly creative and am able to renew myself and transform my experiences.

Type 5 — Investigator: The Intense, Cerebral Type

I am a perceptive, cerebral type. I am alert, insightful and curious. I am able to concentrate and focus on developing complex ideas and skills. Independent, innovative and inventive, I can also become preoccupied with my thoughts and imaginary constructs. I can be detached, yet high-strung and intense. I typically have problems with eccentricity, nihilism and isolation.

At My Best: I am a visionary pioneer, often ahead of my time, and able to see the world in an entirely new way.

Type 6 — Loyalist: The Committed, Security-Oriented Type

I am reliable, hardworking, responsible, security oriented and trustworthy. I am an excellent troubleshooter and can foresee problems and foster cooperation, but can also become defensive, evasive and anxious: running on stress while complaining about it. I can be cautious and indecisive, but also reactive, defiant and rebellious. I typically have problems with self-doubt and suspicion.

At My Best: I am internally stable and self-reliant, courageously championing myself and others.

Type Seven — Enthusiast: The Busy, Fun-Loving Type

I am a busy, outgoing, productive type. I am extroverted, optimistic, versatile and spontaneous. Playful, high-spirited and practical, I can also misapply many talents, becoming over-extended, scattered and undisciplined. I constantly seek new and exciting experiences, but can become distracted and exhausted by staying on the go. I typically have problems with impatience and impulsiveness.

At My Best: I focus my talents on worthwhile goals, becoming appreciative, joyous and satisfied.

Type Eight — Challenger: The Powerful, Dominating Type

I am a powerful, aggressive, self-confident, strong and assertive. Protective, resourceful, straight talking and decisive, I can also be egocentric and domineering. I feel I must control my environment, especially people, sometimes becoming confrontational and intimidating. I typically have problems with my temper and with allowing myself to be vulnerable.

At My Best: I am self-mastering and I use my strength to improve others' lives, becoming heroic, magnanimous and inspiring.

Type Nine — Peacemaker: The Easygoing, Self-effacing Type

I am accepting, trusting, easy going, and stable. I am usually grounded, supportive and often creative, but can also be too willing to go along with others to keep the peace. I want everything to go smoothly and be without conflict, but I can also tend to be complacent and emotionally distant, simplifying problems and ignoring anything upsetting. I typically have problems with inertia and stubbornness.

At My Best: I am indomitable and all-embracing and able to bring people together to heal conflicts.

The Enneagram and Team Effectiveness

In addition to building personal awareness, we also use the Enneagram to improve team effectiveness. Working within natural work groups, we ask individuals to respond to each of the following questions:

- What do others appreciate about your style?
- What is difficult about working with you?
- What do you need to remember when working with people who have other styles?

By using the Enneatype structure, participants are able to answer the questions. Using a model can help depersonalize the feedback and also help increase self and other awareness required to effectively relate to others. Using this structure opens a dialogue about how to work together effectively.

Exercises like the one above are intended to help you stay aware of both strengths and challenges within yourself and others. Moreover, they are designed to help you develop an increased sensitivity to people with differing styles without being restricted by your own biases. As you enhance your ability to respectfully relate to people of different styles, you are also able to improve their impact on stakeholders both inside and outside the company, improving your organization's overall effectiveness.

The Enneagram and Team Roles

We also use a simplified grouping of the nine types to talk about how individuals function and influence performance within a team environment. The nine types are grouped into three team roles. We are assuming that all of these roles are important to high functioning teams. When assigning people to a team, it is important to explicitly consider type in addition to specific professional acumen and skills to ensure that the work of the team will be done effectively.

TABLE 1-2 ENNEAGRAM TEAM ROLES

INITIATORS like to get started and learn as they go along. They like action, diving in, getting engaged and involved (types eight, three and seven).

- Eight: "I'm here, I'll make things happen."
- Three: "Listen to what I have done/accomplished."
- Seven: "I'm here, things will get lively."

COOPERATORS want to take time to find out who the team is, understand the framework, what is behind it, and clarify the expectations, rules and guidelines in more detail. They have more questions about who is in charge of what and explore potential conflict with differing expectations (types one, two, and six).

- One: "I need to organize and fix this."
- Two: "How can I help?"
- Six: "I'm part of the high impact group."

SOLOISTS want to spend some time independently, thinking about a situation and feeling their way to an inner understanding of it. Others may perceive them as being withdrawn, not including others, or even being aloof (types four, five, and nine).

- Four: "I like to find an unconventional, creative solution."
- Five: "I like to observe and understand the patterns and theories."
- Nine: "I like to understand the perspectives of all of the stakeholders and build consensus."

Application

Let's examine a very practical application within an organizational setting. Hilke Richmer used a typing model, specifically the Enneagram, as the foundation to create a leadership development program and wrote about the results for her PhD dissertation. According to Richmer:

> *The purpose of the research was to assess the effects of the Personal Awareness and Effective Leadership Program in a medium-sized utility company in the Midwest United States. To provide middle managers with a unique development opportunity to enhance their awareness of self and others, the company had customized the Personal Awareness and Effective Leadership Program based on the Enneagram in 2009. The program was implemented in 2010.*

She elaborates:

> *The company's organization development team conceived a program that focused on strengthening middle managers' interpersonal effectiveness and leadership versatility. Considering the extensive practical leadership experience of most middle managers and the challenge of actually changing leadership behavior, the team decided on a novel approach. Team members identified the Enneagram, one of the most comprehensive models of personality [leader type] and human development, as an appropriate instrument for the developmental program.*

> *The Enneagram represented an accepted system to support middle managers to develop a better understanding of themselves and others. Therefore, teaching the Enneagram in leader development should foster middle managers' self-awareness and ultimately advance leadership behavior. This research evaluated the effects of the 2010 Personal Awareness and Effective Leadership Program for middle managers on enhancing self-awareness.*

> *As a result of participating in the Personal Awareness and Effective Leadership Program, the company expected leaders to (a) understand the Enneagram and the nine [leader] personality types as identified by the Enneagram, be able to identify their own type, and realize their*

developmental path, (b) apply Enneagram and Situational Leadership knowledge in their leadership to better recognize motivations and values in themselves and others, and (c) become better equipped to consciously self-regulate behavior in leadership situations and communicate more effectively.

Her research concluded the following:

Participants in both cohorts [training groups] found the Enneagram valuable to understand the rationale for their own behavior as well as others' actions and reactions. Participants acknowledged that the Enneagram fostered the understanding of why we behave as we do and also how to best read others. One participant stated that to be an effective leader in today's workforce, you must be able to understand why you are the way you are, so that you can improve.

Richmer's experiment illustrates a crucial step toward building innovative leadership. To begin increasing your capacity for clear decision-making, you must first learn to impartially evaluate and examine the intentional and behavioral patterns in yourself as well as others. The inherent leverage within this simple yet powerful understanding cannot be overstated. It elicits a clarity that will help you make decisions without being governed by the bias of your own perceptions, even as you naturally experience them in any given occasion.

This objectivity is rooted in your ability see your conditioning without preference. It is this nonjudgmental perspective that allows the nuances of experience to persist in the interest of gaining real understanding. When you begin seeing in this way, you can navigate skillfully and execute without the baggage of erroneous expectations.

Applying a typing model can be an exceptionally valuable asset to team building and optimization. One of the critical challenges in working with teams is overcoming the conflicts of interest based on mischaracterization of team members. Such misconstrued perceptions can drain teams of precious energy as time is spent resolving conflict rather than attending to workloads and goals.

Here is an example of an exercise we ask team members to perform based on their type and team role:

- *What is your team composition? How many are Initiators? Cooperators? Soloists? Is there a prominent type within the team?*

- *Which tasks are best accomplished by each type?*

- *What do you need from group members to be most effective? Share your needs with the team.*

- *What ground rules will promote the most effective functioning of this team?*

It is important to note that while assessment can be very powerful, in some cases it is used ineffectively. Whatever typing tool is employed, it should always be used to support and enhance awareness and appreciation of yourself and others. It is unethical to use assessments to pigeon-hole, label, discriminate or disadvantage people. Typing assessments are offered to benefit the individual and the team with personal growth and enhanced team effectiveness. We recommend that you share your Enneagram type with team members and colleagues to improve team and group dynamics. The Enneagram is a very effective tool to improve self-awareness and social interactions.

In summary, this chapter provided a brief introduction and sample of how type models can be used. By harnessing the capacity to see your leader type and conditioning in an objective, nonjudgmental way, you are able to foster better insight in relation to your own experience without the strained effort that can stem from self-bias. You discovered the unique patterns that shape each type are genuine, natural and generally do not change much over time. In the most basic way, they simply reflect who you are most innately. The goal with leader type is to build self-awareness and leverage strengths, not try to change who you are. Understanding the natural conditioning that comes from leader type is a crucial stage in developing leadership effectiveness, and comprehensive innovation within the entire organization.

REFLECTIONS

Using the Enneagram number system, where would you place your leader type?

━━━━━

How have you used other typing tools in the past?

━━━━━

Does this type information help increase your level of awareness regarding your habitual patterns, strengths and growth opportunities?

━━━━━

Do you use this type-based information to guide how you interact with others?

━━━━━

Would an increased use of type knowledge help improve your team effectiveness by promoting discussion among team members about preferred roles and communication styles?

CHAPTER 2:
Developmental Perspectives

Figure 2-1 Five Domains of Innovative Leadership

In the previous chapter, you began exploring a more comprehensive approach to building innovative leadership. You started by simply examining the patterns that comprise your type and serve as a foundation for both personal and professional transformation. You found that you can develop by merely coming to terms with the natural tendencies that encompass your leader type. You can now begin discovering the means to develop greater clarity as well as openly objective leadership style.

The Importance of Developmental Perspective

In this fieldbook we will be talking about ***developmental perspectives*** as a key domain in building innovative leadership. Developmental perspectives significantly influence how you see your role and function in the workplace, how you interact with other people and how you solve problems. The term developmental perspective can be described as "meaning making" or how you make meaning or sense of experiences. This is important because the algorithm you use to make sense of the world influences your thoughts and actions. Incorporating these perspectives as part of your inner exploration is critical to shaping innovative leadership.

Because the concept of developmental perspectives is often overlooked in mainstream organizational literature and programs, and because we believe they are critical to building innovative leadership, we will give a lot of attention to them. We will look at the six most common of those meaning-making approaches in greater detail.

Figure 2-3 Enneagram & Developmental Perspectives

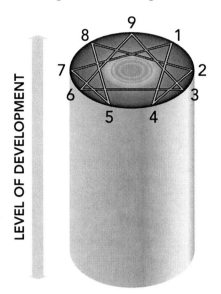

LEVEL OF DEVELOPMENT

In order to connect developmental perspective with leader type, let's look at how these models come together. While leader type is generally constant, you have the capacity to grow and develop your leadership perspective. In fact, leadership research strongly suggests that although inherent leader type determines your tendency to lead, good leaders also develop over time. Therefore, it is often the case that leaders are perhaps both born *and* made. How leaders are made is best described using an approach that considers developmental perspective. Type remains consistent during your life while developmental perspective is grown and is an important differentiator in leadership effectiveness.

We looked for a model to help us identify what the making of a leader looks like so we know how leadership develops in an individual. We can also apply this model to the organizational level to help select and train leaders more effectively. Here are some additional benefits of using a model of developmental perspective:

- It guides leaders in determining their personal development goals and action plans using developmental perspectives as an important criteria.

- It is important to consider when determining which individuals and team members best fit specific roles.

- It helps in identifying high-potential leaders to groom for growth opportunities.

- It helps in the hiring process to determine individual fit for a specific job.

- It helps change agents understand the perspective of others and craft solutions that meet the needs of all stakeholders.

The Leadership Maturity Model and Developmental Levels/Perspectives

Figure 2-2 Maslow's Hierarch of Needs

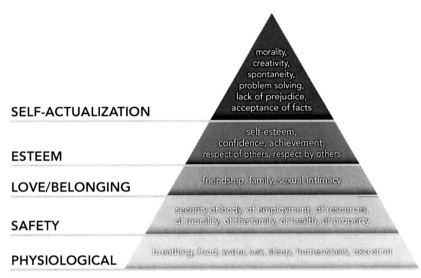

The developmental perspective approach is based on research and observation that, over time, people tend to grow and progress through a number of very distinct stages of awareness and ability. One of the most well-known and tested developmental models is Abraham Maslow's "Hierarchy of Needs." A visual aid Maslow created to help explain his Hierarchy of Needs is a pyramid showing levels of human needs, both psychological and physical. As you ascend the steps of the pyramid you can eventually reach a level of self-actualization.

Developmental growth occurs much like other capabilities grow in your life. Building on your leader type, you continue to grow, increasing access to or capacity for additional skills. We call this "transcend and include" in that you transcend the prior level/perspective and still maintain the ability to function at that perspective. Let us use the example of learning how to run to illustrate the process of development. You must first learn to stand and walk before you can run. And yet, as you eventually master running, you still effortlessly retain the earlier, foundational skill that allowed you to stand and walk. In other words, you can develop your capacity to build beyond the basic skills you have now by moving through more progressive stages.

People develop through stages at vastly differing rates, often influenced by significant events or "disorienting dilemmas." Those events or dilemmas provide opportunities to begin experiencing your world from a completely different point-of-view. The nature of those influential events can vary greatly, ranging from positive social occasions like marriage, a new job or the birth of a child to negative experiences, such as job loss, an accident or death of a loved one. These situations may often trigger more lasting changes in your way of thinking and feeling altogether. New developmental perspectives can develop very gradually over time or, in some cases, emerge quite abruptly.

Some developmentally advanced people may be relatively young and yet others may experiencing very little developmental nuance over the course of their life. Adding to the complexity of developmental growth is the fact that the unfolding of developmental perspectives is not predictably evident along the lines of age, gender, nationality or affluence. We can only experientially sense indicators that help us identify developmental perspective when we listen and exchange ideas with others, employ introspection, and display openness to learning. In fact, most people very naturally intuit and discern what motivates others as well as what causes some of their greatest challenges.

To further examine developmental perspectives we will talk about the assessment tool we use, the **Maturity Assessment Profile (MAP)** and its conceptual support, the **Leadership Maturity Framework (LMF)**. This developmental toolset was created by Susann Cook-Greuter as part of her doctoral dissertation at Harvard. We will use the MAP and the Leadership Maturity Framework as the foundation for our developmental discussion.

The MAP delivers practical information that can be translated into an actionable development plan. This instrument is the most rigorously developed, Harvard-tested, unbiased and reliable perspective measure on the market. The MAP provides unique and personal feedback in addition to perspective description and score. The MAP is also the most sophisticated instrument for identifying and measuring later stage, developmentally advanced leadership. The MAP evaluates three primary dimensions to determine developmental perspective: cognitive complexity, emotional competence and behavior.

> **TABLE 2-1 THREE DIMENSIONS OF DEVELOPMENTAL LEVEL/PERSPECTIVE**
>
> - **Cognitive complexity** describes your capacity to take multiple perspectives and think through increasingly more complex problems. This is akin to solving an algebra problem with multiple variables. For example, a complex thinker is able to balance competing interests like employees' desire for higher pay, with customers' desire to pay low prices and receive good service.
>
> - **Emotional competence** describes your self-awareness, self-management, awareness of others and your ability to build and maintain effective relationships, along with your capacity for empathetic response.
>
> - **Behavior** describes how you act; this dimension generally describes the actions you take.

A sense of time, or time horizon, is another essential feature in the development of perspective. For example, if a leader is limited by their developmental perspective to thinking about the completion of tasks within a timeline of three months or less, then optimally this leader should only be leading a part of the organization that requires short-term tasks. On the other hand, if a leader has the capacity to think and implement tasks with three-year time horizons, then that leader can and likely should be taking on a role that includes longer term tasks. This could be a leader responsible for overseeing the implementation of an enterprise-wide computer system, where the migration may take substantially more time and the process is more complex.

Elaborating on this example, there will be components of the team primarily responsible for the more tactical, hands-on part of the installation and who demonstrate shorter time horizon thinking. Obviously, they are held accountable for certain tasks within the plan but will not be responsible for designing the more strategic portions, nor be charged with the daily decisions that impact the overall budget.

Further still, imagine that one year into the project a key member of the team takes another job and the Project Manager (PM) becomes responsible for finding a suitable replacement. The PM must consider all options when selecting a replacement. The most effective staffing solution for the project will need to account for potential changes over the next 2 years, and how they will impact overall project cost, quality of the final outcome, and team cohesiveness. Time horizons, along with developmental complexity, are directly applicable to innovative organizational decisions.

Detailed Review of Developmental Perspectives

In this section we'll examine the six developmental perspectives most often found in an organizational setting. We will also explore an example of a leader as she develops through some of those developmental perspectives while her underlying type remains unchanged. The following table reflects percentages of leaders testing at each perspective from the David Rooke and Bill Torbert article, *Seven Transformations of Leadership* in Harvard Business Review.

TABLE 2-2 DESCRIPTION OF DEVELOPMENTAL PERSPECTIVES	% of Sample
Diplomat - Demonstrates predominately concrete thinking style. - Hyper-concerned with social acceptance. - Emphasis on conforming to the rules and norms of the desired group. - Imagines that others think and feel the same as they do.	**12%**
Expert - Demonstrates basic abstract thinking. - Concerned with expressing a sense of individuality in sharp contrast to others - Concerned with measuring up to the "right" standards. - Can often appear to be a perfectionist. - Makes constant comparisons with others to gauge identity. - Can often be critical and blame-oriented. - Adept at developing multiple new solutions to problems but not able to determine the best fit solution. - Can begin envisioning short-term time horizons: three months to one year.	**38%**
Achiever - Basic ability to identify shades of gray and see conceptual complexity. - Focuses on causes, achievement, and effectiveness. - Considers others while pursuing their own individual agendas and ideas. - Sees themselves as part of the larger group, yet separate and responsible for their own choices. - Appreciates mutual expression of differences. - Time horizon one-five-years.	**30%**

Individualist - Increased capacity for advanced complex thinking. - Exhibits an ability to appreciate paradox in circumstances. - Begins to value and use rudimentary aspects of intuition. - Beginning awareness that perception shapes reality, including their own. - Self-reflective and investigative of their own personalized assumptions, as well as others. - Understands mutual interdependence with others. - Lives personal convictions according to internal standards. - Style is tenacious and humble. - Longer time horizon: five–ten years.	**10%**
Strategist - Perceives systematic patterns and long term trends with uncanny clarity. - Can easily differentiate objective versus subjectively biased events. - Exhibits a strong focus on self-development, self-actualization, and authenticity. - Pursues actualizing personal convictions according to internal standards. - Management style is tenacious and yet humble. - Understands the importance of mutual interdependence with others. - Well-advanced time horizon: approximately fifteen – twenty years with concern for legacy.	**4%**
Magician/Alchemist - Seeks transformation of organizations not according to conventional goals but according to a higher order. - Has a transforming ability to draw together opposites and initiate new directions from creative tension. - Tends to build their own novel organizations or work on their own to offer their best contribution to humanity. - Seen as visionary leaders. - Time horizon in excess of twenty years	**1%**

Developmental Perspective and Organizational Effectiveness

Developmental perspective not only helps you as an individual leader create your growth path, it is also helpful in improving organizational effectiveness. The key to high performance is to align people and roles considering their developmental perspective. Different functions within the organization are best filled by people at different developmental perspectives. We call this their "fit" for the role, or more precisely, how the qualities associated with their developmental perspective align with specific job's requirements. It is important for both leaders and organizations to support the health of all employees from a developmental standpoint and create an environment where each individual is in a role where they best fit and can move toward their fullest potential.

In order for you to be successful as a leader over the long run, it is essential to understand your proper "fit" within the organization which includes understanding who you are and what you value, where you belong in the organization, and where you belong within the broader team and community stakeholders. Importantly, the goal is not merely to achieve the *"highest"* developmental perspective, rather it is to function effectively in your organization and stakeholder community, while facilitating positive fit among your teams and within your organization. Based on your personal goals and aspirations, you may find that moving to a *"higher"* perspective will allow you to better accomplish your goals.

You can use this developmental model with organizations in several ways:

- Make staffing and succession decisions using developmental perspectives. Try to align people to the roles that have the best "fit" considering developmental perspective along with past performance and technical and industry skills.

- Improving communication skills - apply a general understanding of developmental perspective to guide leaders in improving interpersonal effectiveness. Instead of simply communicating with others as ourselves, we recommend communicating with them based on their level. Understanding the perceptions of others from a developmental standpoint can dramatically improve interpersonal effectiveness. This is true with staff, peers, bosses, clients, family members, as well as other stakeholders.

- Improving management – applying an understanding of developmental perspectives allows a leader to clarify the needs of employees. Expert employees want clear and specific directions and guidelines so they can do their tasks "right". Individualists want the freedom to determine the best approach to accomplishing tasks. Trying to manage these different developmental perspectives using the same approach will result in frustration and lost productivity.

Application

In this chapter, rather than giving an example of a project, we chose to give an example of a person, Jill, who is a composite of multiple people we have worked with as they developed through developmental perspectives. Our intent is to illustrate how a leader progresses through the developmental perspectives and how they find "fit" in jobs aligned with their developmental perspective. We place great importance on developmental level and the leader's ability to take these perspectives as part of building innovative leadership.

Introduction to Jill

Jill is the first child of a young couple. Her mother finished law school when Jill was still a baby and became an attorney at a local law firm. At the time, her father was a chef at a mid-priced restaurant in town. Between the two of them, they made a nice living for Jill and her younger sister, Beth.

A normal child growing up in the Midwest, Jill grew up in quite the typical fashion. Her parents encouraged education and values-oriented life experiences, so she took piano lessons and played sports. She discovered her talent for athletics, particularly soccer, but was also a good pupil who was well-liked by her teachers and fellow students.

Diplomat

*Around age 14, as she entered high school, Jill began to develop around the **Diplomat** perspective. She began focusing on issues such as the different groups at school (nerds, athletes, musicians, etc.), what clothes other kids were wearing, and what accessories were important.*

Jill also began identifying more closely with her peers, specifically the athletes. As such, she pushed her parents to buy her the clothing, accessories and status symbols to match her circle of friends.

She began joining her friends in the teasing of those who were of lower ranked status according to the consensus of other students, specifically the nerds. Jill focused on enforcing that those around her and her group know their status and importance. She kept her own behavior and language within the bounds created by her circle of friends.

Personal appearance became very important to Jill as she came to believe that a significant part of her value was in her appearance. Having the right clothes, hair style, make up and accessories were critical to her and occasionally this created conflict with her parents who apparently failed to recognize their importance.

Jill loved to give advice to those around her about how to fit into their world. Her sister enjoyed Jill's help as she tried to navigate junior high school.

Anytime Jill broke a rule, she felt disappointed in herself as though she was letting down her friends. She was often concerned with what other people thought about her and those thoughts generally dictated her own self-image.

As we'll see in Jill's development, the **Expert** perspective is concerned with doing a good job as defined by a specific organization's standards. Experts appreciate hierarchy, command and control because these structures allow them to easily understand who is setting the standards they need to follow to be successful.

Let's examine the Expert behaviors and transitions by continuing the story of Jill's developmental growth:

Expert

Jill started moving into the Expert stage as she finished high school and entered college at a state school in a neighboring city. She moved into a dorm with some friends from high school, although her roommate was someone she never met. Late night conversations with this roommate, an international student with a very different background from Jill's, pushed her to consider new ideas. While her old friends still held considerable influence, Jill became more aware of her individuality apart from them.

Jill learned intellectually and emotionally through her college experiences. She began seeing the many options before her as she looked at different majors. Her conversations with her roommate become more meaningful as she explored her new identity. She thought more about her role in the world and what traits would help differentiate her from others.

As Jill evaluated her skills, she cemented her belief that she was detail oriented and excellent at math. She fell in love with accounting with its many defined rules and procedures. She quickly became a standout in the department as she studied excessively and roses to the top of the class.

Jill started tutoring in accounting to make a little extra money. She became well known for her expertise in the field as well as her obsessive questioning of those working with her. She was often found asking why someone took a particular action and defending her own answer. Her professors quickly learned that any deduction on one of her papers would result in an email interrogation and explanation about how Jill's response was correct, if not superior to the professor's.

As she finished up her college experience, Jill's competence attracted the attention of recruiters and she was offered several positions. Jill created a pros and cons matrix to evaluate the opportunities, but eventually turned to her parents for help in making her decision. She took their advice and accepted the job at the Big 4 accounting office in the state capital just a couple hours away from home.

Jill settled into her first professional job but did not make friends as easily as she did before. Her first manager seemed to be irritated by Jill's incessant questioning and her initial annual review was not very good. Indeed, her first review was terrifying to Jill as she was told by those she respected that while her work was fine, she was too intimidating and alienating to those around her to be particularly effective. Her pleasant nature had been overtaken by her perfectionism and it was negatively impacting her life.

In response to the feedback, Jill started to pull back a bit in meetings and watch how other people interacted. She continued to receive good marks on her work and her reduced questioning appeared to be well-received. As she evaluated what this meant, she started to transition to the next stage.

Achiever

As one's development continues to progress and unfold in complexity, the next perspective is the **Achiever**. It is worth noting that many senior leaders test at this perspective.

At twenty-five-years old, Jill was working at the nationally known accounting firm. Her altered behavior made her more popular although she still didn't really understand why. However, with her popularity came more invitations to join her co-workers for dinner and drinks. As she spent more time with her colleagues, she started to become aware that her style was not consistent with others.

She hired an image consultant to help her appear more professional as this would help advance her career. The restaurants and bars frequented by the group were often filled with designer clothes and adjacent to a parking lot of BMWs and Acuras.

Jill started thinking about what she wanted out of life and developed a five-year plan. This plan included her goals in several areas of life including: career, house and car, marriage and family, and savings.

For the first time since she was a little girl, Jill started a journal and wrote about her life experience. She appreciated seeing the changes in herself. She started reading biographies as a way to evaluating how other people's choices helped bring about the lives they enjoyed.

Jill decided that she would like to return to school to earn an MBA; she noticed that many of the senior executives in her company had advanced degrees. Returning to school and getting promoted were two of the key goals in Jill's five-year plan.

Once Jill returned to graduate school, it seemed all of her time was spent working or studying. Her reviews improved as she started managing her time to better accomplish her five-year plan. Her task list for each day got a little longer until she was working 60 hours a week minimum; her boss noticed this and Jill was promoted to the next level. The substantial pay increase allowed Jill to buy a house for herself and a garage for her new Audi TT. She was excited about these purchases but had little time to appreciate them. Most of her energy continued to be dedicated to work and school.

Jill often attended training events to learn about the latest GAAP or FASB pronouncements. At one of these events, she met Matthew, an accountant at another firm. As they talked, they found they both value responsibility, family and community. Their courtship was slow as they each worked significant hours but they found time to meet once a week. Jill was delighted as getting engaged was on her five-year plan and Matthew appeared to be just the right fit for her.

After a few years of dating, Matthew proposed. Jill happily accepted and they set a date for another year down the road. Jill's hours at work reduced just a bit as she planned the wedding but she was still effective enough to receive another promotion. At 31, she was making more money than she thought she ever would and was about to marry a wonderful man. Jill didn't think that life could get much better.

The wedding went off without a hitch and Jill sold her house to move into Matthew's place as it was quite a bit bigger than hers. They settled happily into married life with both of their careers going strong.

About five years went by and Jill was still quite happy with her marriage and career. However, the firm she dedicated her entire professional career and much of her life to was experiencing significant financial trouble. Unexpectedly, they laid off her whole department. Suddenly, Jill became unemployed. She was in a state of shock and confusion immediately after the layoff.

People at the **Achiever** perspective are primarily concerned with accomplishing and completing tasks. Their focus has moved away from the mere perfection of each task and toward achieving as much as possible. The Achiever's primary focus tends to be heavily aimed at delivering the desired results. These could be installing a computer system, delivering financial returns to stockholders, exceeding sales goals or raising money for charity. They are often very successful and resourceful, especially if there are clearly presented goals and measurable objectives to achieve.

As one becomes a highly effective Achiever, further growth may move into the next developmental stage, **Individualist**. This perspective tends to be much less common among most typical organizations. Let's proceed further with Jill's narrative:

Individualist

At 37, Jill was out-of-work and disoriented. She had spent fifteen years with the firm that summarily cut her out. She spent the first few weeks after losing her job feeling a bit lost; she was at home all day with no immediate agenda other than figuring out what she wanted to do next. This was a question she never imagined she would be asking herself. Matthew was working even more than his usual 60 hours to attempt to ensure he did not meet a similar fate.

Jill was fortunate that her firm offered outplacement services. Her counselor helped her begin to explore what she wanted in the next phase of her career.

In addition to considering her career, Jill started thinking about what this would mean for her life. She picked up her journal and wrote her thoughts about her motivations and choices. She started thinking about the roles she had made for herself: daughter, employee, boss, and wife.

As the months went by, Jill withdrew somewhat from her social life and became more introspective, trying to make peace with what had suddenly happened. However, filling a need to get up and move, she decided to start taking yoga classes. She recalled wanting to do yoga before but had never found the time. So, she started in and connected with a new group of people.

The individuals in her yoga class were different from her other friends and she enjoyed learning more about them and their perspectives. Jill talked quite a bit with another man in the class, Randy. He was also a business professional so there were similar backgrounds. Randy was laid off several years ago so Jill was able to relate to him. Randy found another job that provided him much greater satisfaction than the one he had left and was able to provide a sounding board to Jill as she evaluated her life.

Jill started to deeply value the opinions of those around her, particularly when they differed from her own. This seemed new to her as she didn't recall input and feedback being so critically important to her before. She was experiencing many things differently as she stretched her mind. She was less focused on her five-year plan and more on what was happening in the moment. Jill started meditating to help maintain a sense of calm and focus. She found that meditation helped keep her mind from wandering and away from her ongoing questioning of what she had done wrong to lose her job.

In conversations with Randy, Jill talked about the different parts of herself and the different roles she played in life. She saw how the different roles had taken over at various points in her life. Specifically, how she had weighted the logical, analytical side so heavily during her career that she had lost the part of her that loved sports and reading books. She talked with Randy and wrote in her Journal about how to rediscover these different aspects of her personality in a meaningful way.

Jill reached out to her family and spent a couple weeks with her parents asking questions about their beliefs and choices. She was amazed to hear their stories about her childhood; she learned things about herself and her parents that she hadn't realized before. For example, as a small girl, she had loved to play in the woods and watch her dad cook. Her family had traveled around the country camping in National Parks. As a child, she had developed a deep love and reverence for the natural world but had forgotten these passions as her focus shifted during her life. In an attempt to reconnect with the passions she had as a younger person, she helped her dad in the kitchen during her visit and was surprised how much she enjoyed slowing down and delving into the different ingredients. It was a sensory, tactical experience that she had devalued during her career when she was focused on all things logical and analytical. She decided to plant a garden in her yard to grow some of her own food. This placed her outdoors allowing her to reconnect with her love of the natural world and with food.

During her time between jobs, Jill began taking time to enjoy being outside. Initially she went to local parks to hike and journal. She began to remember the joy she felt when she was alone in the woods. Over time she started going to a retreat center in the woods where she spent days with her journal and books. She was away from her computer and cell phone for the first time in over fifteen years. She and her dog, Yoda, took long hikes often. Over a period of months, she began to feel more connected to what it seems she had lost during the years of long hours of work and graduate school. She began to have a sense of peace in her life.

As she re-evaluated her perspectives, Jill was becoming more environmentally conscious and beginning to think about and question long-term organizational sustainability. Living in the state capital, she had ample opportunity to join groups focused on sustainability. Her interest in environmental sustainability expanded and she began volunteering her time at a nature preserve.

During this time period, Jill's relationship with Matthew became rocky as he was unable to relate to what Jill was going through. She spent time thinking about why she got married and what Matthew brought to her life. After much thought and frustrated discussion with Matthew about what she was doing with her life, they sought counseling to work out their differences. While they had drifted apart, they were dedicated to each other and recommitted to one another during this process. Both Jill and Matthew agreed to make changes in their relationship including discovering common activities and making time for one another. During the rekindling of their relationship, Jill began to feel the support she needed to explore options other than returning to accounting.

Jill began looking at new career opportunities. She wanted to find work where she could feel satisfied and make a difference in the world. Also, she wanted to work for an organization that was socially responsible. Exploring the worlds of yoga, hiking and environmentalism were wonderfully satisfying to her but none of them would provide the paycheck she needed to survive.

Jill began exploring what she needed to live. She considered downsizing her house, if Matthew would support this choice. She did not want to return to a job that would require her to work so much. She wanted more balance. Her growing awareness of the world around her changed the meaning of things and they became just that: things. She felt weighed down by all she had accumulated and wanted to simplify.

Jill's trip to her parents stayed with her and she developed an enduring and unexpected interest in food and nature. She began trying out recipes and exploring cooking the foods she grew in her garden. She also augmented her diet with food from a local farmer's market. She started buying organic food and cooking healthy meals. She would often invite her new friends over to taste her food. She felt a sense of joy in having another way to connect with friends beyond the fancy restaurants and trendy bars they had hung out in during her years with the accounting firm.

As Jill explored her professional options, she began looking at different ways to combine her professional skills with her passion to make a difference in the world. She decided to take a job as the Director of Finance with a national medical supply company that was socially responsible. This job allowed her to use her financial and leadership skills and also work for a company that impacted society in a positive manner through their socially responsible initiatives as well as their focus on minimizing their environmental footprint.

Additionally, she began teaching cooking classes in an adult learning program and she became involved in the slow food movement. She continued to have friends over to experiment with new recipes that she would share with her adult students.

People who exhibit the **Individualist** perspective demonstrate a much higher level of self-awareness, self-regulation, social-awareness, and relational ability than those at earlier perspectives. They are more likely to think "outside of the box" and often will try to redefine or make sense of "the box" in terms of their own personal experience. Because they are less constrained by conventional thinking, they often develop more creative or innovative solutions to challenges.

As you think about how different levels interact, consider the unique perspective of each level, such as how the Individualist is interested and focused on being out of the box while the Expert needs to use the box to help define the right terms of success. Thus, if an Individualist leader supervises Expert employees, successful outcomes will hinge upon the clear definition of tasks.

We now see Jill break into a very pivotal stage of the developmental path: the **Strategist**. Strategist thinking is effective at balancing all critical areas of decision-making. At this stage, leaders are capable of balancing both short and long-term decisions, maintaining the needs of multiple stakeholders, and effectively weighing the need for structure while remaining flexible and responsive. The strategist is capable of giving clear direction as well as responding to the ongoing stream of new information and the inevitable disruptions to plans. The strategist instills confidence in others while acknowledging their own personal limitations. Let's continue with Jill's story of expanding growth:

Strategist

At age 42, Jill has joined a global consulting firm as a Partner. On a daily basis she is involved in helping leaders and their organizations become more effective and sustainable. Jill and Matthew sold their large house and invested in a modest home with great sun for Jill's garden. They retrofit the house with a gourmet kitchen so that friends can join them for meals cooked with fresh local food. Jill often works from home which fits her lifestyle that now values balance.

She works with others who have similar values who also appreciate the flexibility she provides them. Randy comes by often and is her mentor and friend.

Jill feels a meaningful commitment to her life as she dedicates herself to improving organizational effectiveness of her clients. She also works to create jobs paying fair wages and having a positive impact on the community and the world. She has moved from working as a volunteer to be the Board Treasurer of the nearby nature preserve. She leads the nature preserve to expand their mission to include children's wilderness experiences and creating a community garden. She believes that her volunteer time should have as much impact as possible and board work allows her to meet an organizational need that is not otherwise available to her.

When Jill thinks about her marriage, she is grateful that she and Matthew decided to work through their relationship challenges. She recognizes that while the counseling and personal changes were difficult, he has played a critical role in her life and she still loves him for his willingness to support her during her transition. She is excited to see Matthew make several changes in how he sees himself in the world as a result of their counseling such as his willingness to simplify their living arrangements and move to a much smaller home.

At this stage, Jill has learned to value her own thought processes and time alone enough that twice a year she deliberately spends one week at a cabin in a nearby state park with her Journal. Matthew joins her in this experience during which he hikes and reads. During this time, Jill evaluates what she is doing with her life and what needs to change. She thinks about her different strengths and contemplates if she is overusing any, as she did when she was younger. She appreciates the many opportunities afforded to her to be logical, analytical, creative, strategic, and tactical.

Jill's perspective is moving toward thinking about the global implications of issues. She finds that she is now considering how systems fit together and she wants to reach out to connect *her organization to others in other countries to make the best use of global resources. She is now representing the United States at the World Economic Forum. She is strengthening her network of connections and is eventually offered a role with a global organization. The opportunity comes from an initiative emerging from the World Economic Forum. Her ability to think in a twenty-year time horizon as well as her cultural sensitivity makes her effective in this new role. She begins working closely with the Gates Foundation and other prestigious groups and finds her organization is making a significant impact in areas that are important to environmental sustainability and global peace.*

Jill continues to meditate, run, eat in a healthy manner, and do yoga. She has found that taking care of her body, mind and spirit allows her to function effectively in very stressful situations. Her meditation has worked to strengthen her focus so she is not pulled off track nearly as much by challenges that come up on a daily basis. Additionally, exercising helps her burn off the frustration of the day and she feels refreshed and calm as well as sensing an increase in her stamina.

In summarizing the Strategist perspective, it is important to note that leaders at earlier developmental perspectives can be very effective. The Strategist perspective becomes most important when leading large complex organizations or activities. It is not necessary for a CEO to be solidly grounded in the Strategist perspective if he or she has an advisor who is. Often a CEO role attracts leaders who demonstrate the Achiever perspective while others who have different life goals may fill roles that are less visible in a trade-off that may allow for a greater balance in life.

At this point, Jill's commitments and life conditions do not require a transformation to the Magician stage of development. She is fit to her roles and will likely not continue to develop vertically unless new commitments or evolving life conditions create pressure on her to transform yet again.

The next perspective of development is the **Magician**. The leaders we see with access to this perspective tend to work outside of large corporations, favoring more fluid environments that allow them to have an impact on a broad range of interests. They are effective at leading society transformations.

Our exploration of developmental perspective illustrates that having a deep understanding of perspectives is a critical element when contemplating leadership effectiveness. Though developmental perspectives are less understood when compared with other broadly defined domains of leadership, understanding them is an essential component of innovative leadership.

This chapter provided a brief introduction of a developmental perspective model. This model can be helpful as you determine your personal developmental perspective relative to your personal and career goals. Understanding how to apply this model effectively can greatly improve your communication effectiveness and interpersonal interactions with people who function at different perspectives.

REFLECTIONS

Based on this chapter, how much do you resonate with each of the developmental perspectives described?

Given your current job, is your developmental perspective a good fit?

As you read Jill's story, could you identify two or three people in your life who function at different levels? Given this brief summary, how might you interact with them differently to increase your collective effectiveness?

Does this understanding of developmental perspective give you helpful information about what your personal growth path might include?

CHAPTER 3:

Resilience

Figure 3-1 Five Domains of Innovative Leadership

There are two distinct ways to understand resilience. First, using an engineering analogy, resilience is viewed as how much disturbance your systems can absorb before a breakdown. This view highlights the sturdiness of individual systems. Second, from a leadership perspective, resilience can be viewed as the ability to adapt in the face of erratic change while continuing to be both fluid in approach and driven towards attaining strategic goals. The first definition reflects stability and the second refers to fluidity and endurance. Addressing all aspects of resilience is critical to optimizing it.

The Importance of Resilience

Among the domains essential to leadership, resilience is unique in that it integrates the physical and psychological aspects of leader type and developmental perspective to create the foundation of a leader's inner stability. This foundation enables you to demonstrate fluidity and endurance as you appropriately adapt to ongoing change.

In previous chapters we introduced the qualities that comprise your leader type and the potential you have to enhance your developmental perspective. In examining resilience, we are going to further explore the physical and psychological nuances of both leader type and developmental perspective and how they impact your personal well-being. The underlying premise is this: as a leader, you need to be physically and emotionally healthy to do a good job. In addition to physical and emotional health, the resilient leader also has a clear sense of life purpose and strong supportive relationships. For most people, enhancing resilience requires a personal change.

The Resilience Model

Figure 3-2 Elements of Resilience

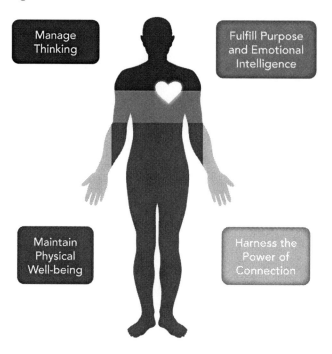

Our resilience approach is based on research by Dr. Susan Kobasa as well as current business research from organizations like Gallup that investigate well-being.

Our model has four categories, shown in Figure 3-2. They are: maintain physical well-being, manage thoughts, fulfill purpose using emotional intelligence, and harness the power of connection. These categories are interlinked, and all of them must be in balance to create long-term resilience.

Leaders we work with often say they are too busy to take care of themselves. There is a balance between self-care and meeting all of our daily commitments. Most people fall short of their goals and over the longer term, you will make choices for your resilience and personal health or against it. Our message here is that creating and maintaining resilience is essential to your success. As you improve your resilience, you will think more clearly and have a greater positive impact in your interactions with others; investing in your resilience supports the entire organization's effectiveness.

TABLE 3-1 KEYS TO BUILDING & RETAINING PERSONAL RESILIENCE

Maintain physical well-being

Are you getting enough:
- Sleep
- Exercise
- Healthy food
- Time in nature
- Time to meditate & relax

Are you limiting or eliminating:
- Caffeine
- Nicotine

Fulfill life purpose and emotional intelligence

Understand what you stand for. Maintain focus. Ask:
- What is my purpose?
- Why is it important to me?
- What values do I hold that will enable me to accomplish my purpose?
- What opportunities do I have in my professional life that help me achieve my life purpose?

Manage thinking

Practice telling yourself:
- Challenges are normal and healthy for any individual or organization
- My current problem is a doorway to an innovative solution
- I feel inspired about the opportunity to create new possibilities that did not exist before.

Harness the power of connection

Practice effective communication:
- Say things simply, and clearly.
- Make communication safe by being responsive.
- Encourage people to ask questions and clarify if they do not understand your message.
- Balance advocacy for your point with inquiring about the other persons' points.
- When you have a different point of view, seek to understand how and why the other person believes what they do in a non-threatening way.
- When in doubt, share information and emotions.
- Build trust by acting for the greater good.

Maintain Physical Well-being

According to Gallup, "Those with high physical well-being simply have more energy to get more done in less time. You are more likely to be in a good mood, thus boosting the engagement of your colleagues and customers."

Physical well-being is something you likely understand and yet give limited focus. Some basic elements include:

- Get enough sleep
- Exercise 6 days per week
- Eat well
- Limit caffeine and alcohol
- Eliminate nicotine
- Meditate and relax
- Take time in nature

While this may seem obvious to you, many people still work with a sleep deficit on a regular basis. There is an increasing body of research supporting the idea that you are less effective when sleep deprived. Additionally, while there is conflicting data, more research is suggesting that it is important to exercise six days per week including aerobics and strength training. Other studies point to the impact of meditation such as Mindfulness Based Stress Reduction (MBSR) programs. In a study that appeared in the January 30, 2011 issue of *Psychiatry Research: Neuroimaging*, "A team led by Massachusetts General Hospital (MGH) researchers report the results of their study, the first to document meditation-produced changes over time in the brain's grey matter… Participating in an 8-week mindfulness meditation program appears to make measurable changes in brain regions associated with memory, sense of self, empathy and [reduced] stress."

One of the key goals in maintaining physical well-being is managing the amount and impact of stress. We define stress as one of several physical or emotional factors that create physiological and/or psychological tension. Tension is normal and adaptive when the autonomic nervous system processes it in a healthy manner. Problems occur only if you do not recover from tension quickly, leading to symptoms caused by reduced immune system functioning.

Key to physical resilience: Build daily routines that help your body recover from stress.

The physiological impact of ongoing stress is often debilitating because of the negative impact on your body's immune system. If your body is not given regular opportunities to recover from the tension associated with stress, the results can range from diminished concentration to anxiety and/or depression to vulnerability to disease, including chronic conditions.

Manage Thinking

It is essential to stay in touch with what is really happening now instead of limiting yourself with beliefs and assumptions based on your past experiences which may no longer be relevant.. Your mental perspective is based on your attitudes, beliefs, and assumptions rather than knowledge. Negative and inflexible thinking prevents your ability to see the big picture and to find creative and alternative routes toward your goal. Your assumptions can diminish your capacity for awareness by holding on to prior beliefs that you think are still true. You may shape your experience into what you think it should be. You may respond to present situations based on your past even when conditions have changed.

Several studies, including a book written by Daniel Todd Gilbert, *Stumbling on Happiness*, support the idea that after a period of adjustment, you return to prior levels of happiness no matter what you tend to endure personally. In building resilience, it is often helpful to develop a broader perspective, keeping in mind that what you are going through is also part of larger cycles. Despite the extremes of your immediate experience, positive or negative, events will balance themselves out over the long term.

Keys to Managing Thinking: Question assumptions, attitudes and beliefs, and actively monitor and redirect your thoughts consistently.

A key area of importance is controlling negative thinking and replacing it with positive thinking. Negative thinking undermines resilience because attention is focused non-productively. By reducing negative thinking, you will have a greater ability to concentrate and think clearly. Examples of negative thinking include:

- Jumping to conclusions
- Not seeing the forest for the trees, often called tunnel vision
- Personalizing, thinking everything is focused on you
- Attributing responsibility and blame to others
- Over-generalizing, applying data from one situation to an unrelated situation
- Assuming what others are thinking instead of asking

An example of controlling negative thinking is when an individual is criticized for their interaction with a stakeholder. The individual might jump to the conclusion that the stakeholder did not value the interactions or their expertise. The individual might take the criticism personally, concluding that their job is in jeopardy. An antidote to these two types of negative thinking, personalizing and jumping to conclusions, is for the individual to ask for more information. They could ask the stakeholder the following questions: "When you commented about this interaction, were you including me in that statement? Is there anything you would like me do differently in our working relationship?"

With this additional information, the individual will be able to correct their thinking and possibly their behavior. They are able to reduce the wasted energy spent on worrying and move quickly to action. This type of interaction takes discipline and courage.

The antidote is not always as easy as stopping a conversation and asking a clarifying question. Dealing with negative thinking is critical because you can waste a great deal of emotional energy in things that are completely unproductive. This energy could be invested in many other areas if you actively address negative thinking.

Because negative thinking can have such a strong impact on resilience, it is critical to build practices that replace negative thinking and mitigate the physiological and emotional impact it has. Areas to consider include building the capacity to:

- Participate in a positive way even when things do not go your way
- Find ways to feel good about your role and about yourself
- Replace negative habits and activities with something positive

When we facilitate workshops we spend a great deal of time on this specific element of resilience. It is an area that you have the greatest control over. Monitoring your thinking does not require extra time or equipment like you might need to enhance your exercise program.

Fulfill Life Purpose While Living Your Values to Fulfill Life Purpose Using Emotional Intelligence

Having a strong sense of life purpose creates a strong foundation for resilience. According to Daniel Goleman's research comparing star performers with average performers in senior leadership positions, he found that nearly 90% of the difference in their performance profiles was attributable to emotional intelligence factors. In leadership roles, emotional intelligence is an important factor in accomplishing life purpose. Key areas of emotional intelligence are:

- Self-awareness
- Self-management
- Social awareness
- Relationship management

The research on Emotional Intelligence (EQ) as referenced in *Primal Leadership: Learning to Lead with Emotional Intelligence* by Daniel Goleman, Richard E. Boyatzis and Annie McKee suggests outstanding leaders have high EQ in addition to high IQ. Emotions impact reasoning and decision-making, and if neglected can derail your ability to implement well-structured plans. Because your emotions are contagious, your ability to manage them impacts those with whom you work. Basically, emotional intelligence addresses your ability to work with others. In leadership roles, your ability to read others and develop strong relationships allows you to accomplish your business goals.

Keys to purpose and emotional intelligence: Have a clear life purpose, develop skills in self-management, and appreciate and work with your emotions regularly. We addressed part of the process of self-management when we talked about managing your negative and positive thinking. This section will focus more on developing a clear life purpose.

By understanding what you stand for, you are much better able to maintain your perspective and focus on the things you care most about. Most people find that when they know what is important to them, they have a much greater capacity to overlook the small stuff. As you clarify your purpose, you may find that things that previously bothered you begin to look like the less important "small stuff." What opportunities do you have in your professional life that helps you achieve life purpose?

In addition to being clear about life purpose, it is critical to have regular activities that contribute to your ability to renew yourself. An activity that many people find helpful is meditation or prayer. Engaging in prayer can help you manage your thought process and also help you connect with something larger than yourself. Renewal contributes significantly to your ability to consistently demonstrate emotional intelligence. According to the book, *Resonant Leadership,* renewing yourself and connecting with others through mindfulness, hope, and compassion are three activities that have a significant impact on your ability to interact innovatively with others.

- Mindfulness: being awake, aware and attending to the world
- Hope: believing that the future you envision is attainable and moving toward your vision and goals while inspiring others toward those goals as well
- Compassion: understanding people's wants and needs and feeling motivated to act on those feelings

Another powerful tool to renew your emotional capacity is performing acts of kindness and service directed toward others. According to *The Economics of Well-being* by Gallup Press (2010), "When we surveyed more than 23,000 people, we found that nearly 9 in 10 report 'getting an emotional boost' from doing kind things for others…throughout the course of our lives, 'well-doing' enhances our social interaction as well as our meaning and purpose. And some studies suggest that it inoculates us from stress and other negative emotions, thus increasing longevity."

Harness the Power of Connection

The ability to interact with other people with awareness, empathy, and skills is vital in building resilience. Because social awareness and relationship management are so important, we are revisiting a key factor previously mentioned in emotional intelligence. The purpose of relationship management as we are discussing it here is to use these skills to understand and work effectively with internal and external organizational stakeholders such as employees, executives, regulators, customers and other important stakeholders.

According to Gallup "Those without a best friend in the workplace have just a 1 in 12 chance of being engaged. Social relationships at work have also been shown to boost employee retention, safety, work quality and customer engagement." We use the term relationship management rather than best friend when we talk about emotional intelligence.

This Gallup research represents a significant shift in how many people look at relationships at work and the importance of developing strong connections. We believe the research is clear: investing your time in connecting with colleagues improves your work and your work environment. We believe it is important to maintain professionalism in business relationships and respect professional boundaries.

The belief that having strong relationships at work sustainably boosts work quality differs significantly from what many experienced early in their careers, where the prevailing attitude was to focus on tasks while at work and build relationships using your personal time. You may have been actively discouraged from developing close relationships with colleagues to avoid being seen as "unprofessional." What do you believe about friendships within the work place? How do these beliefs align with the Gallup research?

A key factor in building successful relationships is communicating consistently in an open and honest manner, and doing what you say. Here are a few tips to improving your communication:

- Say things simply, and clearly
- Make communication safe by being responsive
- Encourage people to ask questions and clarify if they do not understand you
- Balance advocacy for your point with inquiring about the other person's points
- When you have a different point of view, seek to understand how and why the other person believes what they do in a non-threatening way
- When in doubt, share information and emotions
- Build trust by acting for the greater good

Keys to harness the power of connection: Invest time in key relationships and build skills such as communication and empathy that are necessary in relating to others.

Resilience and Organizational Effectiveness

Organizations benefit significantly from having resilient leaders and yet, it is often organizational culture and systems that encourage behaviors at odds with resilience. To bring about true individual and organizational change, leaders must incorporate resilience into the larger picture of leadership development and organizational effectiveness. As an innovative leader, you will develop action plans for transitioning your organization from the status quo to one that supports resilient leaders and workers. As an example, an innovative leader we worked with committed to encouraging employees to negotiate due dates for non-critical tasks. In this case, employees had not been taking personal time off because they felt the need to be "on call" continually even when their tasks did not require this level of availability. Having due dates that appropriately address the criticality of tasks allowed them the flexibility to integrate time for exercise and better work-life balance that resulted in them feeling more energetic and engaged when on the job.

Application

This case study outlines an example of resilience in action and the effect of cultivating it in the midst of professional turmoil. In this case, improvement in resilience allowed employees to remain focused, stay engaged, and maintain productivity and safety standards while reducing the negative physical and emotional impacts of a very challenging time.

Company Profile:

MeadWestvaco, a global packaging company operating in 30 countries, is known for its brands in healthcare, personal beauty care, food and beverage, media and entertainment, as well as home and gardening. The company employs 22,000 people worldwide and serves customers in 100 nations. In 2009, an effort to strategically reduce costs and overhead included plans to close its MWV Calmar facility, (a pump and dispensing manufacturing and distribution operations located in Washington Court House, Ohio. The company consolidated production and equipment with an outside contractor and moved from Washington Court House to Monterey, Mexico. This move offered greater scalability and featured more advanced production equipment and processes for the company and stakeholders.

Challenge/Vision:

Calmar had been a longtime, sizable employer in the southern Ohio town of Washington Courthouse. The company had employed 334 people, many of whom were closely related. Plant closings of this size in a rural area create hardships for workers and their families and can challenge the economic stability of the entire town.

"Thomas Payton, Human Resources Manager, Calmar, Inc., had been working on his master's degree with a focus on developing hardiness and resilience for employees. Still, Payton sought outside help to plan for the closing, including providing support and transition for the employees.

"I was looking for an organization to help facilitate the process of closing the plant and specifically [helping us address] the human resource issues that we were facing," explained Payton. "I had a good relationship with employees and the union and also knew that bringing in someone from outside the company had benefits," noted Payton.

Solution:

Working with an outside firm, Payton and the plant manager developed a plan for employee transition and provided employee coaching during the plant closing process. The Project Team conducted resilience workshops and coached company leaders during the transition. Additionally, the outside firm coached Payton individually on how to manage and lead the group through the changes they were about to experience.

A facilitator from outside the company conducted a workshop for key members of management, hourly employees and some union members in which resilience during change was explored in depth. The goal was to help employees prepare for the transition and plan for their future. Employees were dealing with two different sets of challenges, staying productive while the plant was being closed and concurrently identifying their next career steps. During the workshop and ongoing counseling, they were given tools to help them with both sets of challenges. To deal with the plant closing, they focused on topics like managing their thinking and maintaining strong connections with each other. They were encouraged to explore their own sense of purpose as they considered their next career steps. Managers were also involved in special workshops on how to plan and manage their own transition while supporting their employees and closing the plant in a professional manner.

In addition to resilience training, the Plant Management Team attended monthly sessions where they discussed the challenges they were experiencing and talked about how to cope with them. There were also one-on-one coaching sessions for the Plant Management Team geared toward supporting them during this transition.

"The plant manager and I held meetings in which we acknowledged the grieving process for employees. We spent time talking and listening to individuals' experiences. In effect, we helped to 'mitigate the anger of the experience'," explained Payton.

Results:

Using the resilience tools discussed earlier in this chapter, "MeadWestvaco employees were able to gain a new sense of control during the closing of their plant. As a result, accidents were reduced and the plant made every production and delivery goal, resulting in the plant making a profit for two months longer than Corporate expectations and materially exceeding the capabilities of other plants that were shut down that didn't have resiliency programs" according to Payton.

This chapter provided a brief introduction of how, through building resilience capacity, innovative leaders can increase the capacity of both individual employees and their organizations to achieve their goals. Having the ability to maintain physical well-being, manage thoughts, fulfill purpose using emotional intelligence, and harness the power of connection is critical to being an innovative leader.

REFLECTIONS

Where would you rank your resilience in each of
the four categories?

▰▰▰▰▰▰

How does increased resilience improve your effectiveness
as a person and as a leader?

▰▰▰▰▰▰

What is your biggest resilience challenge?

▰▰▰▰▰▰

Think of areas in your life where you may indulge in negative
thinking then think of an antidote or approach to step away
from the negative thinking and replace it with positive thinking.

▰▰▰▰▰▰

If you are overly challenged, how can you build
resilience skills to reduce your anxiety?

▰▰▰▰▰▰

If you are over qualified and we feel bored, what can you take
on that will offer additional challenge to your work life?

▰▰▰▰▰▰

What are you doing that supports or hinders building
and maintaining friendships? What steps could you take
to initiate or deepen those connections?

▰▰▰▰▰▰

If you were to make progress on your biggest resilience
challenge, what small step could you commit to over the next
month that will help you improve your resilience?

CHAPTER 4:

Situational Analysis

Figure 4-1 Five Domains of Innovative Leadership

Though much of building innovative leadership is based on an in-depth examination of your personal and professional experience, understanding the background or context of that experience is equally important. Consider that your experience isn't merely a collection of willful personal expressions, events and random happenstance; rather, it is fundamentally shaped by the background interplay of your individual attributes, shared relationships and involved institutions. In other words, experiences not only unfold as depictions of your unique personal views, but are also culturally filtered through your interpersonal relationships with others, objectively affected in your behaviors and socially distributed through your networks and technological systems.

The Importance of Situational Analysis

The nature of human experience is more than simple personal expression. More fundamentally, it includes a background of forces that also shape and impact every moment of your reality.

Every moment of experience is influenced by a mutual interaction of self, culture, action and systems. All four of these basic dimensions are fundamental to every experience we have and mutually shape them in all circumstances. Situational analysis involves employing the four-dimensional view of reality we show in Figure 4-2 to balance the realities you face in the most comprehensive way possible. We refer to these four qualities as self, action, culture and systems. This balancing without favoring elements is an important part skill for innovative leaders.

A multi-faceted approach provides a more complete and accurate view of events and situations. Leaders often take a partial approach to changing organizations. They over-emphasize systems change with little or no consideration to the culture or how their personal views and actions shape the content and success of the change. Situational analysis enables you to create alignment across the four dimensions on an ongoing basis.

Integral Model and Situational Awareness

Figure 4.2- Integral Model

American born philosopher Ken Wilber developed a conceptual scheme to illustrate the four basic dimensions of being that form the backbone of experience. His Integral Model provides a map that shows the mutual relationship and interconnection among four dimensions where each represents basic elements of human experience. This interconnection is shown in Figure 4-3.

When you practice situational analysis, you are cultivating simultaneous awareness of all four dimensions. Let's look at an example. This is a sample narrative taken from *Integral Life Practice* (Wilber et al) that will give you a more experiential description of how these dimensions shape every situation in your life.

Example: *"Visualize yourself walking into an office building in the morning…"*

Self (*Upper-Left Quadrant, "I"*)*:* You feel excited and a little nervous about the big meeting today. Thoughts race through your head about how best to prepare.

Culture (*Lower-Left Quadrant, "We"*)*:* You enter a familiar office culture of shared meaning, values, and expectations that are communicated, explicitly and implicitly, every day.

Action *(Upper-Right, "It"):* Your physical behaviors are obvious: walking, waving good morning, opening a door, sitting down at your desk, turning on the computer, and so on. Brain activity, heart rate, and perspiration all increase as the important meeting draws nearer.

System *(Lower-Right, "Its"):* Elevators, powered by electricity generated miles away, lift you to your floor. You easily navigate the familiar office environment, arrive at your desk, and log on to the company's intranet to check the latest sales numbers within the company's several international markets."

A crucial part of building innovative leadership is the development of your capacity to be aware of all elements of reality in any given moment and identify misalignments. Even though you cannot physically see the values, beliefs and emotions that strongly influence the way an individual colleague perceives himself/herself and the world, nor a group's culture, emotional climate or collective perception, they still profoundly shape the vision and potential of leaders to innovate.

Alignment and Influence

We will use an alignment model to describe how using Situational Analysis as a tool of innovative leadership allows you not only to make more informed decisions but also helps you optimize performance within yourself, your teams and the broader organization. The alignment of all dimensions is the key to optimizing performance.

Let's explore alignment across the four dimensions. We start with self, culture, action and systems and explore how these dimensions create an aligned system that is cohesive and integrated. Figure 4-3 shows the image of an aligned system and the following section describes how the dimensions are aligned.

Figure 4.3 Alignments across Dimensions

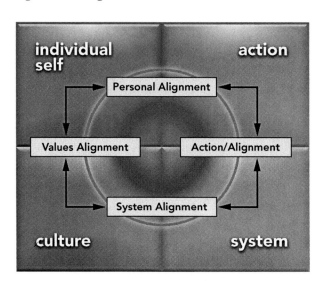

■ *Personal Alignment:* the ongoing process of coordinating your self-dimension (identify, thoughts, emotional intelligence and perspective taking) with your action dimension (behavior, role function, execution, individual performance) to create a sense of personal integrity within yourself and inspire trust in others.

■ *Action Alignment:* the ongoing process of coordinating your action dimension (behavior, role function, execution, individual performance) with the organization's system dimension (network, structure, system processes, and organizational results) to create recognition for you and efficient and effective organizational results.

■ *System Alignment:* the ongoing process of coordinating system dimension (network, structure, system processes, and organizational results) with the culture dimension (organizational values, communication and climate) to increasing functional efficiency among organizational culture and systems.

■ *Values Alignment:* the ongoing process of coordinating the culture dimension (organizational values, communication and climate) with the self-dimension (identify, thoughts, emotional intelligence and perspective taking) to create a sense of individual alignment with organizational values that promotes a feeling of fit for the individual and a sense of value based leaders for the organization.

While we have not drawn the arrows on the diagonal, when the dimensions are aligned as shown in Figure 4-3, all dimensions reflect balanced alignment.

Application

Following is an example where a Project Manager used the Situational Analysis model during the implementation of an enterprise-wide employee recognition system that impacted 30,000 workers. The project focused on assessing options and selecting and implementing a solution that would improve employee engagement. The project manager considered all dimensions to ensure the solution chosen was as comprehensive as possible, and successfully implemented the system to create long-term impact on employee engagement, client retention and satisfaction. The PM worked with an implementation team consisting of client employees and members from the team that sold the recognition system.

- **Personal Alignment:** In agreeing to take on the project, the Project Manager (PM) evaluated commitment to this assignment by checking personal values against the actions that would be required for implementation. The PM was personally committed to employee recognition as a tool to increase associate engagement while positively impacting customer enthusiasm and business results. The project was well aligned with the PM's personal belief about how companies recognize employees in ways that are personally meaningful to the employees, linking performance to organizational strategy, culture and systems. This project was designed to accomplish all of these outcomes. The PM could take the actions required to perform the role and maintain alignment between self and action.

- **Action Alignment:** The Project Manager continually verified that the PM and implementation team actions were aligned with the organizational systems. Additionally, the PM verified that all participants were in roles for which they were well qualified. The PM worked within the established systems and structures of the organization. Understanding and working within the prevailing systems of the organization allowed the implementation team to function effectively with minimal disruption to the existing structure.

- **System Alignment:** The system here is defined as the performance management systems and processes within the organization as well as the new recognition system. The PM evaluated how the recognition system would align to the existing performance management systems and company culture, as well as the team selecting options with similar alignment. A key part of the implementation process was tailoring the recognition system to fit the culture and align with the multiple existing performance management systems. One way the recognition system reflected the culture was to create an option to recognize employees for living the company values. By the time the recognition system was launched, it was closely aligned with the company culture and integrated into the existing performance management systems.

- ■ **Values Alignment:** In this project, the culture is defined as the culture of the client organization. The PM evaluated the connection between self-dimension and company values. As mentioned in action alignment, the PM values employee recognition. The company expressly states they value people, honesty and integrity, coaching and feedback and several others. The PM's values were aligned with the company values, allowing the PM to act with a sense of integrity in that the client would not ask her to do anything that conflicted with her values.

The project manager was aware of the four dimensions concurrently and paid attention to the impact created during the initial alignment. By giving balanced attention to all dimensions and ensuring alignment, the PM led a team to successfully complete a project ensuring immediate and long-term impact on the organization. The project received positive feedback after its launch because of the ease and success of the release. Additionally, it is being used extensively by employees with over 15,000 recognition messages sent within the first six months.

Increased situational analysis helps you as an innovative leader to create holistic solutions by removing misalignment among the four key dimensions. The process of deliberately evaluating the four basic dimensions of any experience can provide you with a tool to identify potential disconnects that could waste resources and cause great frustration for you and your employees. From a leadership perspective Situational Analysis will allow you to have greater impact because you have taken the deliberate step to align all the dimensions.

This chapter has provided a brief introduction to the integral model, which addresses the four dimensions that are present in all of our experiences. The goal of Situational Analysis is to create alignment across the four dimensions through deliberate action within each one. Deliberately focusing on alignment is a key lever to implementing innovative changes that allow your organization to thrive.

REFLECTIONS

Do you work for an organization that is aligned with
your personal purpose and values?

■■■■■■

How often do you take time to consider how you think or
feel about a task before you move forward?

■■■■■■

Where do you see misalignments between what you value and
how you act because of pressures from your organization?

■■■■■■

Where do you see misalignments between what your
organization says it values and the systems it has put in place
(such as performance management and compensation)?

■■■■■■

If you were to start using the integral model when making
big decisions what would your first step be?

CHAPTER 5:
Leadership Behaviors

Figure 5-1 Five Domains of Innovative Leadership

In previous chapters we have explored the inner world and qualities associated with an innovative leader, including leader type and developmental perspective. Your type and developmental perspective reflect aspects of your being while resilience connects your interior lives and actions that promote your overall well-being. We further explored the four dimensions of experience and how Situational Analysis can promote alignment across the dimensions to increase efficiency and effectiveness along with a sense of personal integrity.

The Importance of Leadership Behaviors

Let's now shift our focus to the more actionable craft of leadership as defined by behaviors and skills. In this chapter, we will examine the place of observable leadership skills and behaviors and hard skills and their associated behaviors. Leadership skills and hard skills are critical to success, and serve as objective performance measures of innovative leadership. Hard skills fall into two primary categories: industry related knowledge, skills and aptitudes; and functional knowledge, skills and aptitudes. Leadership behaviors are the result of knowledge, skills and aptitudes specifically related to the craft of leadership. We will be using the term leadership behaviors in this fieldbook when referring to leadership knowledge, skills and aptitudes and the resulting behaviors. Both hard skills and leadership behaviors are critical to building innovative leadership. The balance between the importance of hard skills and leadership behaviors will shift as the leader progresses in the organization with leadership skills and behaviors becoming increasingly important with career advancement.

Leadership behaviors are important because they are the objective actions the leader takes that impact organizational success. We have all seen brilliant leaders behave in a manner that damages their organization and we have seen other leaders continually behave in ways that promote ongoing organizational success. Effective leadership behavior drives organizational success and conversely ineffective leadership behaviors drive organizational dysfunction or failure. In this chapter we will look at the leadership behaviors associated with innovative leadership.

An example of the need for both hard skills and leadership behaviors is a hospital CEO client. To be successful, this CEO must possess the hard skills in hospital administration to understand how the hospital operates and the leadership behaviors to be able to effectively lead. If either of these sets of skills is missing, the leader and the hospital are at risk of failure. Early in his career, a mastery of hospital administration set him apart from his peers. As he progressed into the senior leadership ranks and ultimately to the role of CEO, his use of leadership behaviors became his primary focus while he never lost the need for hard skills.

The Leadership Circle Profile™ and Leadership Behaviors

There are several different ways to discuss leadership from a skills perspective as demonstrated by Peter Northouse in his recent book on leadership.

> *There are several strengths in conceptualizing leadership from a skills [actions] perspective. First, it is a leader-centered model that stresses the importance of the leader's abilities, and it places learning skills at the center of effective leadership performance. Second, the skills approach describes leadership in such a way that it makes it available to everyone. Skills are behaviors that we all can learn to develop and improve. Third, the skills approach provides a sophisticated map that explains how effective leadership performance can be achieved.*
>
> *Peter G Northhouse, Leadership Theory and Practice,*
> *Sage Publications 2010, p. 66.*

We will use an assessment model to discuss leadership behaviors just as we used the Enneagram to measure personality type and the MAP to measure developmental level. We use the Leadership Circle Profile (LCP) and the associated framework from the Leadership Circle® to explore leadership behaviors.

The Leadership Circle Profile is an assessment tool that collects feedback from the leader's boss, boss's boss, peers, and subordinates to provide a 360-degree perspective of the leader's performance along with the leader's self-assessment. High quality leadership behavior assessments are solidly researched and measure behaviors shown to correlate to leadership effectiveness and to important business outcomes. The Leadership Circle Profile is a unique competency-based 360-degree assessment and includes belief systems and assumptions that underpin a leader's behavior. This tool integrates well with other tools such as the Enneagram leadership type model and MAP, developmental perspective model, in a way that provides great insight to leaders.

Although the Leadership Circle Profile incorporates elements of type, beliefs, and developmental perspective, we are positioning it in this fieldbook to address leadership behaviors. The purpose of going into detail here is to give insight into the actual behaviors associated with innovative leaders.

As the reader using this fieldbook, you may choose to use the assessments we have discussed (Enneagram, MAP and LCP) or others. We recommend the suite of tools we have discussed because they work well together and in many cases the theories underpinning the assessments are also aligned. If you select other tools, we recommend you research the interconnections and also conflicts that may arise from the information provided.

As with the discussion on the Enneagram assessment, it is critical to use an assessment tool effectively to receive the benefit from it. Unlike the Enneagram, most leaders do not share their individual scores with teammates. The LCP is designed to provide detailed information to the leader to support development. For many leaders these results show weaknesses that they would like to keep private. If the organization is using a 360-assessment, it will be important to set expectations in advance to define who will see the data and how it will be used. It should be positioned in a way that supports participants answering honestly and leaders using the resulting scores to improve their performance.

The Leadership Circle Profile (LCP) Behaviors

Figure 5-2 The Leadership Circle Profile

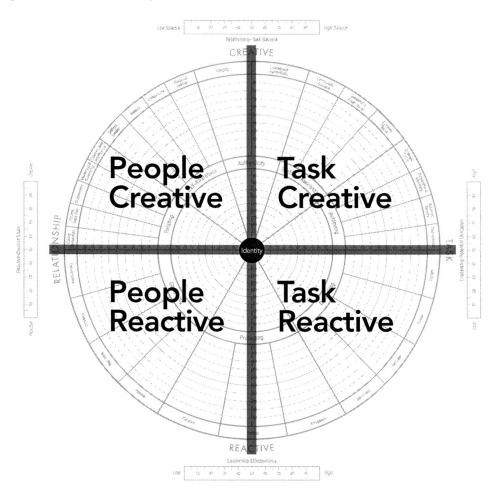

The Leadership Circle measures key dimensions of leadership shown in the inner circle in Figure 5-2. The sub-categories are then shown in the outer circle. These are broken into four key dimensions: people creative, task creative, people reactive and task reactive. These four categories are created by drawing a line through the circle horizontally to separate the creative and reactive dimensions. The second line is drawn vertically to separate the people and task dimensions.

The top of the circle behaviors are Creative behaviors:

- Relating
- Self-awareness
- Authenticity
- Systems Awareness
- Achieving

These behaviors reflect proactive action which is referred to by the Leadership Circle as "Creative." These behaviors reflect behaviors associated with setting strategic direction and inspire people to accomplish goals.

The behaviors in the bottom half of the circle are reactive behaviors. They reflect *inner beliefs that limit effectiveness, authentic expression, and empowering leadership.* These dimensions reflect behaviors associated with following direction or reacting to circumstances as they arise rather than setting direction and creating the conditions for success. These behaviors include:

- Controlling
- Protecting
- Complying

The creative and reactive dimensions are then split on the vertical axis between people and task behaviors. People behaviors are associated with the actions leaders take to build themselves and their people such as relating and self-awareness. The task behaviors are actions leaders take associated with the work of running a business such as systems awareness and achieving.

The blend of the four dimensions required to be innovative will depend on the situation and the organization. It is important to understand the behaviors associated with innovative leadership and also be able to flex your own leadership behaviors to match what is required by the organization. The most effective leaders and organizations demonstrate behaviors heavily weighted on the creative end of the scale. The balance between task and relationship will depend in part on the role of the leader within the organization. Strong leaders have the capacity to perform both people and task related roles well.

According to the *Leadership Circle Participant Profile Manual*, 2009 Edition published by the Leadership Circle, "These competencies [behaviors] have been well researched and shown to be the most critical behaviors and skill sets for leaders." Table 5-1 was adapted from the *Leadership Circle Participant Profile Manual*, 2009 Edition, published by the Leadership Circle.

TABLE 5-1 LEADERSHIP CIRCLE PROFILE DIMENSION DEFINITIONS

The Creative Leadership Behaviors reflect key behaviors and internal assumptions that lead to <u>high fulfillment, high achievement leadership</u>.

The **Relating** Dimension measures leader capability to relate to others in a way that brings out the best in people, groups and organizations. It is composed of: - Caring Connection, - Fosters Team Play. - Collaborator - Mentoring and Developing - Interpersonal Intelligence	The **Self-Awareness** Dimension measures the leader's orientation to ongoing professional and personal development, as well as the degree to which inner self-awareness is expressed through high integrity leadership. It is composed of: - Selfless Leader - Balance - Composure - Personal Learner
The **Authenticity** Dimension measures the leader's capability to relate to others in an authentic, courageous, and high integrity manner. It is composed of: - Integrity - Authenticity	The **Systems Awareness** Dimension measures the degree to which the leader's awareness is focused on whole system improvement and on community welfare (the symbiotic relationship between the long-term welfare of the community and the interests of the organization). It is composed of: - Community Concern - Sustainable Productivity - Systems Thinker
The **Achieving** Dimension measures the extent to which the leader offers visionary, authentic, and high accomplishment leadership. It is composed of: - Strategic Focus - Purposeful and Visionary - Achieves Results - Decisiveness	

The **Reactive Leadership Styles** reflect inner beliefs that *limit effectiveness, authentic expression, and empowering leadership.*

The **Controlling** Dimension measures the extent to which the leader establishes a sense of personal worth through task accomplishment and personal achievement. Dimensions include: - Perfect - Driven - Ambition - Autocratic	The **Protecting** Dimension which measures the belief that the leader can feel safe and establish a sense of worth through withdrawal, remaining distant, hidden, aloof, cynical, superior, and/or rational. Dimensions include: - Arrogance - Critical - Distance
The **Complying** Dimension measures the extent to which the leader gets a sense of self-worth and security by following the direction of others rather than acting on their own intentions and wants. Dimensions include: - Conservative - Pleasing - Belonging - Passive	

Leadership Behaviors and Organizational Effectiveness

Effective leadership behaviors drive effective organizations. As we build on the Situational Analysis model, effective leaders' behaviors, also referred to as actions in the Situational Analysis model, are one of the four dimensions. If these effective behaviors or actions are aligned with the other dimensions, then the whole system is impacted by who the leader is and how the leader behaves. According to the alignment component of the Situational Analysis model, effective leaders align self and actions to create personal alignment; they align self and cultures to create values alignment; they align their actions and systems to create action alignment; and they align cultures and systems to create system alignment. If the leader's behaviors or actions are ineffective and they have created alignment, the entire system will be ineffective. If their behaviors are ineffective and the system is not aligned, they will still cause organizational dysfunction. If, on the other hand, the leader is behaving in a manner that supports the organization and creates alignment across the dimensions, the entire organization will benefit. The behaviors in the Leadership Circle Profile that are most effective are those represented by the creative dimensions: relating, self-awareness, authenticity, systems Awareness, and achieving.

Application – Case Study

A consulting firm was hired by the centralized IT Department of a global manufacturing company to work with their new CIO. The firm provided coaching and consulting support including:

- Facilitating strategic planning sessions
- Identifying the strengths and weaknesses of leaders
- Coaching leaders to increase individual effectiveness
- Improving leadership team effectiveness
- Identifying guiding principles associated with organizational success supporting organizational restructuring

The consultant administered the LCP assessment and found that the leaders worked in a way that would be considered reactive. The new CIO was creative according to the LCP assessment and wanted his team to demonstrate similar behaviors. He believed the entire organization needed to demonstrate more creative behaviors to accomplishing the organization's strategy. The consultant used the results of the LCP assessment as the foundation for education and leadership coaching.

The CIO revised the IT Department leadership performance evaluation process to formally appraise the leadership behaviors he believed his leaders needed to demonstrate for his organization to be successful. The updated performance management system evaluated leaders on both the results they achieved and the leadership behaviors they used to deliver these results.

He also undertook an extensive process of identifying the guiding principles that would serve as the foundation for the culture change. This process involved facilitated sessions where the leadership team identified the key beliefs and values about how the IT organization would operate. They then created action plans to implement necessary changes to create system alignment between the culture and systems. We point out the multiple changes the CIO made because he is an innovative leader and understands that changes must happen across the four dimensions associated with Situational Analysis to sustain behavioral change.

To focus on the leadership behavior portion of the project, each leader took the LCP. The consultant consolidated the individual leader scores into a team score to allow the CIO to see the overall leadership team behaviors. The composite chart showed:

- The group scored high on the reactive behaviors associated in the complying dimension such as passive and belonging. These scores indicated challenges with accomplishing creative results as they are associated with leaders who are waiting to be told what to do. This data helped the CIO to identify some key behaviors that put his ability to accomplish his goals at risk. Some of the behaviors were a result of the leaders themselves and some of the behaviors were a product of the culture his predecessors had created.

- The group scored low in many of the creative dimensions that are important to success such as achieves results. This data gave the individual leaders important information for improving their effectiveness. It also provided data to the overall leadership group and the CIO about how the leaders worked together and where their behaviors needed to improve.

The organization benefitted from this process by:

- *Increased self-awareness of individual leaders drove behavioral changes.* Each leader was able to see how he or she was perceived by others: boss, boss's boss, peers, and subordinates. The 360 part of the assessment was very helpful in giving each leader a clear and quantifiable picture of possible issues identified by others. For many leaders, there were significant surprises. These surprises became very important as the leaders learned about possible pitfalls and areas where they excelled. The consultant met with each leader and created a leadership improvement plan that focused specifically on behavioral changes. The consultant then met on a regular basis with each leader to support their development. As an example: One leader scored a 1 (on a score of 1-100) on Achieves Results. He came to understand that while he perceived himself as a high performer, his peers did not. This data was an important wake-up call that he needed to make changes and make them quickly.

- *Increased awareness of individual to group dynamics.* Because the consultant consolidated the team scores, each individual was able to identify areas where his or her individual style differed from that of the team. In some areas, these differences explained strains in relationships individuals had with one another. Each individual was able to evaluate his or her fit within the team. Where areas of concern appeared, the coach added the required behavioral changes to the leader's behavioral change plan.

- *Increased awareness of group dynamics.* The leadership team looked at the collective scores and determined what they liked about how they operated as a group and what they would like to change about the dynamics within the group. The consultant facilitated a leadership team- building process to define new behaviors and rules of engagement that supported increased team effectiveness and the creation of a better working environment. A leader's individual behavior often impacted organizational performance across multiple teams.

While the initial Leadership Circle profile scores were low, in the bottom 25% on some key areas, the organization was able to make significant changes over the short-term and the long-term. The use of the Leadership Circle Assessment tool was very important to the new CIO because it gave him important information about key areas for improvement among his leaders. The assessment results allowed him to quickly address the most immediate gaps and opportunities, and then develop a systematic plan to make longer-term changes.

This chapter has provided a brief introduction to how leadership behaviors fit within the overall innovative leadership framework. Leadership behaviors are objective and measurable actions. Understanding the behaviors associated with innovative leadership, as reflected in the Leadership Circle Profile, creates the foundation for you to examine your own behavior and determine where you are functioning as an innovative leader and where you would like to make changes.

REFLECTIONS

If you were to receive feedback on your leadership competencies, where would you excel?
Where would you fall short?

■■■■■■

What percentage of your behavior would an outside observer rank as creative? Reactive?

■■■■■■

Do you prefer task focused activities? Relationship focused activities? What is the percentage split you would assign to each?

■■■■■■

How do you use your understanding of leadership behaviors to select people to work for your organization?
To develop your team?

| 1 Create a Compelling Vision of Your Future | 2 Analyze Your Situation & Strengths | 3 Plan Your Journey | 4 Build Your Team & Communicate | 5 Take Action | 6 Embed Innovation Systematically |

Learn & Refine

SECTION II

Building Innovative Leadership Capacity

In Section I we defined and explained the five key domains of innovative leadership. Now you are ready to move to Section II: "Building Innovative Leadership Capacity." This is the interactive section of the fieldbook containing exercises, worksheets, reflection questions and client examples. It is designed to provide a step-by-step process to support you in developing your own innovative leadership capacity. This book has been tested with clients as well as hundreds of working adults participating in an MBA program. It has been tested and revised over five years to create a process that makes a high impact on leader's capacity.

The process steps are:

- Create a compelling vision of your future
- Analyze your situation and strengths
- Plan your journey
- Build your team and communicate
- Take Action
- Embed innovation systematically

The comprehensiveness of these exercises coupled with reflection exercises will give you the insight into yourself and your organization necessary to make substantive personal change. While this process appears linear, we have found that when leaders work through these steps they often return to earlier parts of the process to clarify and sometimes change details they had originally thought were correct. The structure of our process will continue to challenge you to refine the work you have accomplished in prior tasks. First ideas are often good ones, but when you work with this tool you will find insight coming to you every step of the way. We encourage you to continue to test your ideas and feel comfortable going back in the process for further refinement.

The time you spend working on the fieldbook portion of the book is an investment in your development. If you are engaging deeply in the process it will likely take you three to six months or longer to complete. Whether managing both personal and organizational change, or internal change alone in the context of an organization that you cannot or do not want to change, reflection and thorough evaluation are required. This reflection will take time and is critical to your growth. We strongly encourage you to engage in the process with as much time and attention as possible. The value you ultimately take from this process is closely linked to the time you invest.

CHAPTER 6:

Create a Compelling Vision

Figure 6-1 Innovative Leadership Development Process

The first step in starting your development process is cultivating a sense of clarity about your overall vision which can also be summarized as your direction and aspirations. The intention behind your aspirations fuels both personal and professional goals, as well as a sense of meaning in your life. When your actions are aligned with your goals, they drive the impact you create in the world-at-large. As you move forward in the visioning process, we will guide you to begin thinking about individuals or groups who inspire or have a significant influence on you.

Simply put, your vision and aspirations help you to decide where best to invest your time and energy. Clarifying your personal vision and aspirations helps you define a manner of contributing to the world that authentically honors who you are. Your vision and aspirations further help you clarify what you want to accomplish over time. This can be any time span that resonates especially for you, whether in the short-term—as in one to five years—or perhaps a longer time-horizon, such as the span of your lifetime. Once you clarify your own, unique, personal vision, it will become the foundation for the ensuing change process. Knowing your vision and values ensures that you are precise about your goals and can better align your behavior to your aspirations.

As part of the visioning process, it is important to consider the context of your leadership role, your organization or employer. If you are clear about your personal vision, you can evaluate where and how you fit within that organization. On the other hand, if your vision differs significantly from what you do and how you work, the additional information will guide you to finding a role that is a better fit (this transition may not happen in the short term). By knowing your vision and aspirations, you are equipped with information that helps you align your life energy with the work you do.

In addition to creating a well-defined vision, it is also important to be clear about your motivation. It is the combination of vision and desire that will enable you to optimize your potential. Without sufficient desire combined with solid vision and understanding of your current capabilities, you are likely to struggle when progress becomes difficult.

The focus of this fieldbook is on innovating leadership and organizational transformation, therefore it provides an array of tools applicable to addressing a wide range of approaches to personal change required to support leadership change. This change process and tools differ from many others by directing you through an exploration that accounts for both your unique, individual experience while simultaneously considering the groups and organizations in which you belong. People from all walks of life play important leadership roles that range from leading a family to leading a volunteer organization to running a major corporation. And though the differences in organizational scope, scale, or purpose require different skills, there are common principles that consistently serve as the foundation for leadership. We will elaborate on some of those common principles throughout each exercise.

Tools - Exercises

The first two exercises come from the *Fifth Discipline Field Book* by Kleiner, Roberts, Ross, Senge, and Smith. They will guide you in identifying what is most important to you and how to direct your life. First you will define you vision, what is most important to you, your values and how to accomplish your vision. You will then consider what you want to do professionally as well as the type and extent of the impact on the world you foresee in your future. The first tool offers a set of questions for you to consider when clarifying your vision.

It is important to note that many people will complete this exercise and still not have a clearly articulated vision. The visioning process is iterative in nature, a process of self-discovery, and the exercises in this book will serve as the foundation for a longer process that may take considerably more time to complete. These exercises will serve as a starting point; you will likely refine your vision as you progress through the book based on the information you learn about yourself. For many people, their vision evolves over time, changing as they gain experience and as their introspective process matures.

To begin the process of defining your personal vision, complete the following exercise from the Fifth Discipline Fieldbook.

Define Personal Vision

Follow the steps defined below:

Step 1: Creating a Result.

Imagine achieving a result in your life that you deeply desire. For example, imagine that you could live in an ideal environment, or enjoy a desired level of personal relationships. For the moment, gently ignore how "possible" or "impossible" the intended outcome of your vision seems. Picture yourself accepting the results of the full manifestation of this result into your life.

Now, write or sketch the experience you have imagined, using the present tense, as if it is happening now.

- What does it look like?
- What does it feel like?
- What words would you use to describe it?

Step 2: Reflecting on the First Vision Component.

Now pause and consider your answer to the first question. Did you articulate a vision that is close to what you authentically want? You may find yourself experiencing various levels of resistance to achieving your vision. There may be a variety of reasons why you found it hard to do.

- I cannot have what I want
- I want what someone else wants
- It doesn't matter what I want
- I am afraid of what I want
- I don't know what I want
- I know what I want, but I can't have it at work

Step 3: Describing Your Personal Vision.

Again, answer the following questions using the present tense as if your vision is actually occurring in the immediate moment. You can use the categories below as a general guideline. Continue until you have filled the pages with a complete picture of what you wants.

Imagine achieving the results in your life that you deeply desire. What would they look like? What would they feel like? What words would you use to describe them? You are going into further detail for the vision you articulated earlier in this exercise.

- **Self-Image:** If you could be exactly the kind of person you want to be, what qualities would you have?
- **Tangibles:** What material things would you like to own?
- **Home:** What is your ideal living environment?
- **Health:** What is your desire for health, fitness, athletics, and anything to do with your body?
- **Relationships:** What type of relationship would you like to have with friends, family, and others?
- **Work:** What is your ideal professional or vocational situation? What impact would you like your efforts to have?
- **Personal pursuits:** What would you like to create in the arena of individual learning, travel, reading, or other activities?
- **Community:** What is your ideal vision for the community or society you live in?
- **Other:** What else would you like to create in other arenas of your life?
- **Life Purpose:** Imagine that your life has a unique purpose fulfilled through your interrelationships, what you do, and the way you live. Describe that purpose, as another reflection of your aspirations.

Step 4: Expanding and Clarifying your Vision.

If you are like most people, the choices you put down are a mixture of selfless and self-centered elements. People sometimes ask, "Is it all right to want to be covered in diamonds, or to own a luxury sports car?" Part of the purpose of this exercise is to suspend your judgment about what is "worth" desiring, and to ask instead: Which aspect of these visions is closest to your deepest desire? To find out, you expand and clarify each dimension of your vision. In this step, go back through your written list of components of your personal vision: including elements your self-image, tangibles, home, health, relationships, work, personal pursuits, community, life purpose, and anything else. If you have not yet addressed these elements and they are important, you may consider adding them now.

Ask yourself the following questions about teach element before going on to the next one.

- If I could have it now, would I take it?

Some elements of your vision don't make it past this question. Others pass the test conditionally: Yes, I want it, but only if…" Others pass, and are clarified in the process.

People are sometimes imprecise about their desires, even to themselves. You may, for instance, have written that you would like to own a castle. But if someone actually gave you a castle, with its difficulties of upkeep and modernizations, your life might change for the worse. After imagining yourself responsible for a castle, would you still take it? Or would you amend your desire: "I want a grand living space with a sense of remoteness and security while having all the modern conveniences.

- Assuming that I have this in my life right now, what does it ultimately bring me?

This question catapults you into a richer image of your vision, so you can see its underlying implications more clearly. For example, maybe you wrote down that you want a sports car. Why do you want it? What would it allow you to create? "I want it," you might say, "for the sense of freedom." But why do you want the sense of freedom?

The point is not to denigrate your vision thus far – it's fine to want a sports car – but to expand it. If the sense of freedom is truly important to you, what else could produce it? And if the sense of freedom is important because something else lies under that, how could you understand that deeper motivation more clearly? You might discover you want other forms of freedom, like that which comes from having a healthy figure or physique. And why, it turns, would you want a well-toned body? To play tennis better? Or just because you want it for its own sake? All those reasons are valid, if they're *your* reasons.

Divining all the aspects of the vision takes time. It feels a bit like peeling back the layers of an onion, except that every layer remains valuable. You may never discard your desire to have a sports car, but keep trying to expand your understanding of what is important to you. At each layer ask yourself once again: If I could have it, would I take it? If I had it, what would it bring me?

This dialogue shows how someone handled this part of the exercise:

My goal, right now, is to boost my income

What would that bring you?

I could buy a house in North Carolina.

And what would that bring you?

For one thing, it would bring me closer to my sister. She lives near Charlotte.

And what would that bring you?

A sense of home and connection.

Did you put down on your list that you wanted to have more of a sense of home and connection?

[Laughs] No, I didn't. I just now realized what is really behind my own desires.

And what would a sense of home and connection bring you?

A sense of satisfaction and fulfillment.

And what would that bring you?

I guess there's nothing else – I just want that. [Pause] I still do want a closer relationship with my sister. And the house, And, for that matter, the income. But the sense of fulfillment seems to be the source of what I am striving for.

You may find that many components of your vision lead you to the same three or four primary goals. Each person has his own set of primary goals, sometimes buried so deeply that it's not uncommon to see people brought to tears when they become aware of them. To keep asking the question, "What would it bring me?" immerses you in a gently insistent structure that focuses you to take the time to see what you deeply want.

After defining and clarifying your vision, it is time to consider your personal values. The combination of these two exercises will help you create the foundation of what you want to accomplish and the core principles that guide your actions as you accomplish your vision.

Checklist for Personal Values
from *Fifth Discipline Fieldbook* exercise by Charlotte Roberts

When you consider part of your vision, and something inside you says, "That's really not me," most likely you have felt a pang from a deeply help personal value.

Values are deeply held views of what we find worthwhile. They come from many sources: parents, religion, schools, peers, people we admire, and culture. Many go back to childhood; we take on others as adults. As with all mental models, there's a distinction between our "espoused" values – which we profess to believe in – and our "values in action," which actually guide our behavior. These latter values are coded into our brains at such a fundamental level that we can't easily see them. We rarely bring them to the surface or question them. That's why they create dissonance for us.

As literature and spiritual guides warn us repeatedly, individuals should beware of the temptation to let their values slip when times get tough. Organizations should doubly beware. If your organization values honesty, that means it should show employees the financial books – even when the books are embarrassing. If your organization believes that employees are your most important asset, it means that your first strategy in difficult times will not be layoffs. You may eventually have to lay people off, but it will be considered carefully because it contradicts your organization's values in action.

PERSONAL VALUES CHECKLIST

- Achievement
- Advancement and promotion
- Adventure
- Affection (love and caring)
- Arts
- Challenging problems
- Change and variety
- Close relationships
- Community
- Competence
- Competition
- Cooperation
- County
- Creativity
- Decisiveness
- Democracy
- Ecological awareness
- Economic security
- Effectiveness
- Efficiency
- Ethical practice
- Excellence
- Excitement
- Expertise
- Fame
- Fast Living
- Fast-paced work
- Financial gain
- Freedom
- Friendships
- Growth
- Having a family
- Helping other people
- Helping society
- Honesty
- Independence
- Influencing others
- Inner harmony
- Integrity
- Intellectual status
- Involvement
- Job tranquility

- Knowledge
- Leadership
- Location
- Loyalty
- Market position
- Meaningful work
- Merit
- Money
- Nature
- Openness and honesty
- Order (tranquility/stability)
- Personal development
- Physical challenge
- Pleasure
- Power and authority
- Privacy
- Public service
- Purity
- Recognition from others
- Relationships
- Religion
- Reputation
- Responsibility & accountability
- Security
- Self-respect
- Serenity
- Sophistication
- Spirituality
- Stability
- Status
- Supervising others
- Time away from work
- Truth
- Wealth
- Wisdom
- Work quality
- Work under pressure
- Work with others
- Work alone
- Other: _____

Step 1: Define what you value most: From the list of values (both work and personal), select the ten that are most important to you – as guides for how to behave, or as components of a valued way of life. Feel free to add any values of your own to this list.

Step 2: Elimination: Now that you have identified ten values, imagine that you are only permitted to have five. Which five would you give up? Cross them off. Now imagine that you are only permitted four. Which would you give up? Cross it off. Now cross off another to bring your list down to three. And another, to bring your list down to two. Finally, cross off one of your two values. Which is the one item on the list that you care most about?

Articulation: Take a look at the top three values on your list.

- What does each value mean, exactly? What are you expecting from yourself, even in bad times?

- How would your life be different if those values were prominent and practiced?

- What would an organization which encouraged employees to live up to those values be like?

- Does the personal vision you've outlined reflect those values? If not, should your personal vision be expanded? Again, if not, are you prepared and willing to reconsider those values?

- Are you willing to create a life in which these values are paramount, and help an organization put those values in action?

Putting Vision into Action

After defining and clarifying your vision and values, the next step is to reflect on how to put these into action. You will consider the things you care about most coupled with your innate talents and skills to determine what about your current life you would like to refine or even change. You are probably passionate about specific interests or areas within your life; if you're really fortunate, you will enjoy opportunities to participate in one or more of those areas.

The purpose of this exercise is to consider how best to incorporate your passions into how you make a living. It is also likely that you have passions that will always remain in the realm of hobbies. The main point of the exercise is to move closer to identifying your passions and expressing them in as many areas of life as possible.

In our experience, part of figuring out what you want to do is paying attention to what you find profoundly interesting. Those interests simply revealed themselves in the course of your daily interaction with peers and colleagues, and quite frequently at business functions. They are reflected in whatever you find yourself reading; they even displayed themselves in the context of more casual occasions, and are often seen in activities shared among personal friends.

This is the type of exercise that appears very simple on the surface, and may be something you revisit annually in order to refresh what is genuinely important for you. We find that periodically revisiting these exercises allows you to nurture your sense of continual clarity about your direction. We have worked with both graduate students and clients who have found this type of iteration provides a foundation for clarifying their direction as they grow and develop. With everything they tried (false starts and all) they discovered a deeper truth about themselves that helped get closer to what they found to be their most authentic passions. Some of those passions were incorporated into careers and other passions helped shape their personal lives.

Putting Vision into Action Exercise

Step 1: Answer the three questions by compiling a list of answers to each.

- What are you passionate about? This will come from the prior exercise and should now be a rather concise answer.
- What meets your economic needs?
- What can you be great at?

Note – your answers to these questions should reflect your values from the Personal Values Checklist.

Step 2: Review your answers and identify the overlaps.

Step 3: Harvest the ideas. Based on the overlaps, do you see anything to think about incorporating in what you do or how you do your work? This could mean adding an additional service line to an existing business or allocating a portion of your work time to a project that is aligned with your values.

An example of this is a client who, based on significant reflection, learned he valued giving back to the community in a way that he was not doing. He was the CEO of a technology firm. He stepped back from this role a bit to build a community support function into his business. His passion was offering computer training for returning veterans. He found a way to address a local talent shortage and give back to the veterans who risk their lives to preserve our way of life. His passion for service to the community along with his professional skills affords him the ability to follow his passion and still run a successful business. In the process of following his passion, he is building the workforce in his community and building his reputation as a civic leader and successful entrepreneur.

Defining Vision Based Actions

Figure 6-2

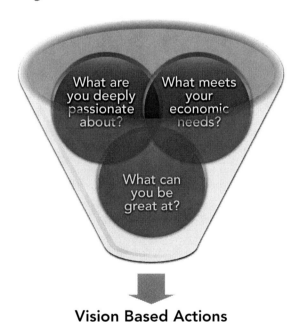

Vision Based Actions

Now that you have developed your vision and values and determined possible next steps to putting your vision into action, it is time to further clarify your direction using reflection questions. These questions are organized by quadrant to reflect the four native domains introduced in Section I. Our definition of innovative leadership: "Leadership is a process of influencing people directionally and tactically, affecting change in intentions, actions, culture and systems" refers to affecting change in intentions, actions, culture and systems. These questions are arranged to help you explore each of these domains. The questions for "What do I think/believe?" reflect your intentions. The "What do I do?" questions reflect your actions. The "What do we believe?" questions reflect culture. The "How do we do this?" questions reflect systems. Thus, we designed this exercise to help you start practicing innovative leadership as you create your vision and define your direction.

TABLE 6-1: QUESTIONS TO GUIDE THE LEADER AND ORGANIZATION

What do I think/believe?

- How do I see myself in the future? What trends do I see around me that impact this view? Have I considered how these trends impact the way I want to contribute?
- How does my view of myself impact me? Am I inspired by my vision? Terrified?
- How do I see myself within the larger environment? This can range from my family, the company, to the global environment.
- After doing the exercises, what is my vision?
- After doing the exercises, what are my values? What do I stand for? What do I stand against?
- What are the connections between my business vision and my personal mission, passion, and economic goals?

What do I do?

- How do I gather input from key stakeholders to incorporate into my vision (family, business, self)?
- How do I research trends that will impact my industry so I can understand my future placement and how to navigate potential transitions in my industry?
- How do I synthesize the competing goals and commitments to create a vision that works for me in the context of the communities I serve (family, friends, work, and community)?
- How do I develop my vision taking the greater economic conditions into account?
- What do I tell others about my vision? Do I have an "elevator speech"? Is it something I think is inspirational?

What do we believe?

- How does my personal vision fit within the larger context of my family, my community my industry or my job?
- How do I create a shared belief that my vision will help the organization succeed within the larger community and also help the community succeed?
- What do we believe we stand for as an organization? How should we behave to accomplish what we stand for (guiding principles/values)? Do my values align with the organizational values?
- How do I reconcile differences between my values and those of my organization? How will these differences impact my ability to develop toward my vision and goals?

> **How do we do this?**
>
> - How do I monitor the organization's impact on my vision? How do I honor my vision when helping define/refine the organizational vision?
> - What is our process for defining/refining changes to our shared vision for the organization and other systems I function within? What is our process for clarifying and documenting our values? How do I ensure that my values are aligned with our guiding principles?
> - Who gives me feedback on their perspective of my progress? How often? What form would I like this feedback to take?
> - What measures help me determine progress toward my vision and values? How do I track and report progress to these goals? Is my behavior supporting the organizational goals? Are the organizational goals supporting my goals?

To tie the developmental perspectives in Section I to the exercises, we will give examples of answers completed from the most common developmental perspectives: Expert, Achiever, Individualist, and Strategist. This section is intended to help you start to recognize different developmental perspectives in yourself and others.

Analysis by Developmental Perspectives

At the **Expert** perspective, as a leader, you are likely to establish a vision that focuses on leveraging expertise. At this level of development, values will reflect the rules and norms of the primary group such as church, family, or colleagues.

At the **Achiever** perspective, as a leader, you are likely to create a vision that focuses on what you can and will accomplish over a five year time horizon, generally measured in material terms such as job title and salary. You will measure the value of your contribution and status you achieve.

At the **Individualist** perspective, as a leader, you are is likely to create a vision that considers life purpose and what you will contribute to the world over a 10-15 year period. This is likely to shift from external measures, such as job title, to a more internal sense of personal fulfillment, including increased universal value or how you would like to conduct yourself in the world. You may start to care more about inclusion, diversity, and social responsibility, evaluating how our actions contribute to what we value most. This is the stage where leaders really start to connect values and actions.

At the **Strategist** perspective, as a leader, you are likely to consider and develop concrete scenarios for a 15-25 year plan as well as your future legacy. You will have much more clarity about what you value, having incorporated those values into your actions through the Individualist perspective. Your concerns will broaden to a larger group; you may find yourself thinking of the global impact of your vision and actions. You will be positioned to transform organizations on a large scale and may find yourself concerned with interconnecting systems and how things fit together. At this perspective you may also be considering significant changes, and may find yourself wondering if you are thinking too big. You will also be thinking heavily about what you value beyond work, things like the quality time you spend with your family or charity organizations.

Stories and Examples

In the next section we will provide examples of how these tools have been used. Jill is a character drawn from our collective experience with several clients of Metcalf & Associates. We also have the story of Bob, the Executive Director of a non-profit organization; Carl, the CEO of a family owned mid-sized business; and Bruce, the Director of a large hospital system in the Midwest. We will share the stories of each of these individuals in the following chapters to give you a realistic flavor of how different leaders use this framework in a variety of situations. Each individual tailored the six step developmental process to meet their own unique, personal and professional goals.

Sample Responses for Jill as a Strategist

Let's examine Jill's process for developing her vision. We use Jill to illustrate use of the exercises from the strategist point of view. This serves two purposes: first, to demonstrate how one might complete the exercise and second, to give insight into the developmental perspective of strategist thinking. Through our client work and teaching we found that having examples of how each perspective uniquely considers these exercises to be especially insightful in personal growth process. We have tried to capture Jill's internal thought process in these exercises in a way that is rare in a business context, but helpful for the purpose of personal development.

Introduction to Jill

At age 42, Jill has joined a global consulting firm as a Partner. On a daily basis she is involved in helping leaders and their organizations become more effective and sustainable, and act responsibly to behave as positive corporate citizens. Jill and Matthew sold their large house and invested in a modest home with plenty of sun for Jill's garden. They retrofit the house with a gourmet kitchen so that friends can join them for meals cooked with fresh local food. Jill often works from home which fits her lifestyle that values balance. She works with others who have similar values who also appreciate the flexibility she provides them. Randy comes by often and is her mentor and friend. Jill tests as a Strategist leader. To read Jill's full development story, please refer back to Chapter 2 – Developmental Perspectives.

Jill's Process of Creating a Compelling Vision

We will now walk through Jill's answers to 1 or 2 questions from each quadrant in **Table 6: Questions to Guide the Leader and Organization.** The table contains an exhaustive list of questions to appeal to a broad range of readers. You will likely find that a few of these questions best fit your own personal situation. Please focus on the questions that seem the most relevant. Simply follow along with Jill to answer the questions for yourself or select the questions that fit your current situation.

Jill's Reflection Questions

What do I think/believe?

■ *How do I see myself in the future?*

I see myself as a person who can significantly contribute to helping leaders and their companies function more effectively and sustainably. For me, this includes: providing reliable products and services to customers at a fair price; paying workers fairly and providing benefits where possible; paying stockholders or owners a fair return for their investment and risk; being a positive impact on the communities in which we operate. I believe that how I behave while accomplishing this goal is very important. I am committed to being wise, compassionate, peaceful, fair, open minded, honest, grounded, and trustworthy.

I take time to develop my employees and serve my community through my professional and volunteer activities. I also hold a strong spiritual faith that gives me peace and a sense that there is some order in the world even if I do not see it personally.

There are also parts of my vision that I am not sharing here. They include my spiritual goals, physical fitness goals, and family goals. While I believe these are all critical to living a balanced and happy life, I am not sharing them in this journal because they are very personal to me.

◼ *How does my view of myself impact me? Am I inspired by my vision? Terrified?*

I am definitely inspired by my vision. If I accomplish what I see as my vision of the future – I will leave the world, the people, and plants better for my presence. This legacy involves businesses, individuals, and the community. My work touches all of these sectors directly. I am proud of my vision and it tends to drive me forward.

I'm aware of my skills and talents as well as my deficiencies. At times I probably see the deficiencies as bigger than they are and the strengths as things everyone can do. I realize this that this distorted perception clouds my judgment, even if it is on the side of humility. Through my regular meditation and journaling as well as work with an experienced coach, I am making a conscious effort to value myself more accurately. If I undervalue myself, I will not set a realistic vision and I will never reach my potential. If I overstate my abilities too much, I may get discouraged and stop short of my potential – or maybe I will actually grow more – who knows?

◼ *How do I see myself within the larger environment? This can range from my family, the company, to the global environment)?*

I see much of my contribution to the world through my paid work and volunteer work. I work for a global consulting firm that is focused on organizational improvement and sustainability. I want this organization to make a significant impact on how client organizations operate responsibly in a manner that allows them to be profitable and also sustain the health of their stakeholders for future generations. If we are successful, we will impact people on all parts of the planet.

Beyond the work vision, I see myself as a person who respects each individual with whom I come into contact. I see my work and my kindness impacting the world in a positive way.

What do I do?

■ *How do I gather input from key stakeholders to incorporate into my vision (family, business, self)?*

My vision is evolving after wondering what I should really do with my life. I continually get feedback from my husband, colleagues, friends, and clients, as well as from within myself during reflection about what seems to be working and what isn't. This feedback can come in the form of recognition, frustration, or praise. At this point in my life, I tend to be very introspective and am listening to my own inner guidance a great deal. I am finding this quite helpful and continue to be aware that many people believe they are following their inner guidance and yet can still have significant blind spots that interfere with clear, well aligned actions. I want to check in with those I trust to make sure I am grounded and realistic.

■ *How do I synthesize the competing goals and commitments to create a vision that works for me in the context of the communities I serve (family, friends, work, and community)?*

I have gone through a very deliberate process to create a vision for myself and my personal contributions. This has been an ongoing process rather than a one-time activity. While some people may grow up knowing what they wanted to do in the world, I certainly did not. What I am doing now did not even exist when I was a child.

I believe that we benefit from refining, if not significantly revising, our vision as we continually learn and grow. I found my own vision to be constantly changing and growing rather than being static. The visioning process is some combination of what appear to be opposing activities; creating a plan and yet also being willing to change the plan as I learn more. Thus, I plan and revise my vision periodically. In this way, vision becomes something more organic that shows itself over time. I like this approach because I could not have selected my current vision even 10 years ago as I would not have predicted accurately what would be happening in my life nor the opportunities I would have available.

So, creating my vision is like the flow of waves – some information coming in and some reaction to the information going out. In any event, I gather information from those around me; I experiment with new behaviors or new ideas. As I experiment, I gain more information. This self-reinforcing cycle is ongoing as I continue to learn and refine. In the learning cycle, I have an opportunity to really learn, refine, and make great progress in areas I would never have imagined.

An important note about my process: part of my information comes from external sources, like the people around me, and some the information comes from within. I make time to think, reflect, and pay attention to my thoughts and feelings. This reflection time allows me to evaluate if I am doing what I want to do and also if I am being the person I want to be. Meditation is an important practice for me because it provides a structure and time that promotes reflection, clarity and peace of mind.

What do we believe?

■ *How does my personal vision fit within the larger context – my family, my community, my industry, my job?*

Matthew is very supportive of my vision and we share similar values. Doing these and similar exercises over the years has helped us to strengthen our foundation as a couple.

My personal vision is highly aligned with my organization. It is evolving and the leadership team is very mindful of our culture and values, and how they impact the organization. As it grows, we are taking more time for me to ensure listening to the values and concerns of others, and integrating them into the company beliefs. We find that people of similar values are attracted to our company and those who differ significantly simply are not.

■ *What do we believe we stand for as an organization? What do we believe about how we should behave to accomplish what we stand for (guiding principles/values)? Do my values align with the organizational values?*

We stand for creating effective, sustainable organizations that serve as positive global citizens (act responsibly). We have created a set of guiding principles that define how we will work together. My values are well aligned with these guiding principles. The challenge for us will be preserving the effectiveness of those principles through appropriate attention to them as we continue to grow. We want to do this without creating onerous burden or unnecessary structure.

How do we do this?

■ *Who gives me feedback on their perspective of my progress? How often? What form would I like this feedback to take?*

Part of my feedback comes from my husband Matthew. I really trust his judgment. He has my best interest at heart and is willing to give me candid feedback. He has been focused on his own development for many years so he has a strong sense of what I stand for.

For my business, I look at the standard performance measures such as growth and profitability. I've also decided to use a 360° assessment tool that measures individual performance and organizational culture. We will implement this assessment this year. It will provide us valuable information about how we are working as a leadership team and will give me important information about how others perceive my behaviors. Because it is a 360 assessment, I will see how people at different levels within the organization see me.

■ *What measures help me determine progress toward my vision and values? How do I track and report progress to these goals? Is my behavior supporting the organizational goals? Are the organization goals supporting my goals?*

I will review my progress annually in December. This discipline will help me maintain sufficient focus on my progress while giving me time to do the other activities in my life as well. During this process I decide if my vision and values should be refined. I also look at my performance against business goals and personal goals. I review journals to remind me about my performance over the year.

The company has an annual planning process where we evaluate our progress during the past year against high level goals. We then confirm our mission, vision and values. We can refine these on an annual basis where appropriate. We then create goals and success measures for the next year. This process also includes an "external scan" where we consider customer input, employee input, economic trends and forcasts.

Introduction to Bob

Bob is a recent client who agreed to collaborate in telling his story. His focus was personal development with some organizational transformation. Bob was the Executive Director of a highly successful non-profit during its rapid growth phase. They went from a small local organization into an internationally recognized accrediting organization under his leadership. He tells his story in his own words to give one example of how a reader may choose to apply the tools.

Bob worked with an advisor who provided coaching and consulting support focused primarily on leadership development and traditional consulting interventions associated with management consulting.

Bob: My goal [in the coaching and consulting process] was to sharpen what I see as the most important tool for achieving the objectives of my organization — myself. My philosophy is that no matter how effective I am as a leader, I can always be better. My experience with self-directed development had been unsatisfactory. Sure, I read all the latest business books, attended management seminars and the like. Ultimately, I found myself encountering the same roadblocks and making similar mistakes as before. I reasoned that if I wanted to see significant development, I would need a skilled coach. You don't become a great chef by winging it in the kitchen; you study under a great chef.

The goal of this engagement was to help Bob increase his leadership effectiveness. Soon after the coaching began, the organization began to experience a shift in focus. The coaching engagement expanded into a coaching and consulting project; the opportunity arose to use the organizational transition as a window to help the client see how a later stage counterpart might address the issues he faced. This approach gave Bob an opportunity to reflect on his actions as compared to how another person would approach those same issues. By exploring potential solutions and providing him with the chance to process the differences between them, he was able to both enhance the organizational solutions along with his own development.

Bob: The best mirror for my development is examining what challenges me in my work environment. Having the ability to practice new behaviors in these real world situations was critical in my understanding of how I was leading the organization and how I could adopt better ways to lead.

I benefitted from mentoring in both worlds: the principles of better leadership, and the actual decisions and behaviors of a better leader. So, on the one hand, I was receiving experienced executive coaching and on the other, this was placed from the point-of-view of a greater developmental perspective. That went beyond the problem I was having with self-directed development, that all those books and lectures, didn't translate well into all the real work situations I was encountering, at least not at the moment I was encountering them. With a developmental and executive coach, the two were combined to guide behavior and insight, right at the times they were needed.

Additionally, the structure of the coaching and consulting allowed us to ensure we were tending to key activities from an integral perspective. We created a risk assessment and transformation plan based on an integral frame of reference. This plan served the leader's development, the organizational culture, the mission, vision, processes and structure. The combination of these activities created a system of reinforcement for the leader to grow and shaped an organization that could likely sustain changes and meet the stated goals.

Bob: This organization-based planning put me ahead of the curve in the leadership I was providing. Having a broader perspective put me at least one step ahead of everyone else, and helped me to bring everyone into a common vision. Even when things came out of left field, I had much more grace under pressure.

Challenge and Vision:

Since its inception, the organization has enjoyed rapid growth. The staff increased from one employee (Bob) in 2001 to 6 employees in 2006 and then to 16 in 2008. At the same time, the budget grew from zero to low-six figures to well into seven figures. Without a cohesive operational structure or a well thought out strategic plan in place, initiatives were sometimes more reactive rather than proactive. To ensure continued growth and success, a more formal structure and plan were needed.

In times of growth, communicating goals and objectives as well as the plan to reach them are particularly important. Without strong communication, employees, management and board members will often times find themselves with differing or even contradictory areas of focus. The challenge was to create a structure and processes that would better position this organization for the future.

Bob: I started my first day on the job with a borrowed card table and folding chair, with $20,000 in seed money, no income and no way to get paid. But, it was the right mission at the right time and I was determined to make it work. I introduced two lines of service to the community that we served that directly supported the mission: hospital accreditation and care provider education. Both of these services became big successes, rapidly growing us from zero revenue to a seven figure revenue organization. After a couple of years of feeling like I was constantly trying to hang on to a bucking bull, I was searching for an effective way to put into place a structure that could support continued growth with less pain.

Bob's Process of Creating a Compelling Vision

The vision and values definition process for Bob included both increasing capabilities and health at his current development perspective while simultaneously facilitating the potential to grow into greater perspectives. He focused on the following domains:

- Love
- Health
- Mission
- Passion
- Security
- Spirit
- Service

His professional vision included making lots of people's lives significantly better by doing an exceptional job at meaningful, customer service oriented work. Additionally, he is continually growing and learning, using his gifts to their fullest, embracing a more positive point of view, earning sufficient income to be financially responsible for family and others, and engaging actively in spiritual growth.

Bob: It is fascinating how closely the work I was doing to clarify my life mission paralleled the work to clarify the mission of the organization. They weren't the same goals, but the more success I had in defining and realizing the one set, the more success I had in realizing the other set. I had been drawing some kind of artificial line between what I defined as my "personal" goals and my goals as an organizational leader. But the truth is that the ultimate success comes from the development of the holistic and balanced man. Trying to say that personal goals around mind and body had no relationship to the realization of the organization goals was an illusion. The better the man, the better the leader.

Bob defined how he wanted to function as a leader. He looked at specific leadership competencies based on The Leadership Circle Assessment he completed. About 18 months into the process, he began using a series of structured exercises to clarify his personal life mission at a deeper level.

During the annual planning process, the client led a strategic planning session with his board. They collectively created the mission, vision, goals, and expected outcomes. The information from this session was the foundation for much of the consulting work.

Introduction to Carl

Carl was a client who agreed to collaborate in telling his story. His focus was personal development in service of transforming his family-owned business. Carl is the 3rd Generation CEO of a highly successful mid-sized family owned business. He tells his story in his own words to give one example of how a reader may choose to apply the tools.

Carl purchased a 91 year old business from his father after working for the company for 14 years. He is now faced with the challenge of carrying on the legacy of success in a changing economic time while navigating the dynamics associated with family and long tenure leadership that helped build the company well before he was involved in the business.

Advisor: I met Carl at a class I taught on Building Transformational Leadership that explored leadership through the lens of developmental theory, specifically using the Mature Adult Profile (MAP), created by Susann Cook-Greuter.
We scheduled an initial call where we agreed to start a small project where Carl would take the MAP assessment, a second test called the 360° assessment, (The Leadership Circle Profile) and engage in coaching.

Carl: Coincidentally, I had been interviewing candidates who would help me develop a vision, mission and business plan. I had attended a COSE (Council of Small Enterprise) strategic planning course at Cleveland State University but still wanted someone with experience to walk me through the process. After attending the Advisor's seminar, I realized that she was promoting more than just a vision, mission and business plan, but rather an organizational transformation through leadership development. The vision, mission and business plan were part of the package, but not the driving factor. When working with someone at this level, it is critical to have the right "energy" between the teacher and the student. Luckily for me, we were a match. While the other candidates brought their skills to the table, I wasn't overly enthused about the possibility of working with them.

So that the reader can gain perspective from my comments, I will offer a brief corporate history and my involvement with the company. The company was founded in 1918 as a typewriter repair company. In the late 1920's, my grandfather started an office supply and furniture company which merged in 1932. In the late 1950's, my father, John, joined the organization as a sales representative. In the early 1970's, the company began selling copier equipment. We also opened our second location. The organization continued to grow and in 1988 we opened our third location. In 1992, I joined with the goal of learning the organization from the ground up. My employment began in the warehouse: stocking shelves, pulling orders and delivering office supplies.

After several years of warehouse and distribution work, I moved to the furniture division where I was responsible for furniture installations and repairs. Following that, I spent time on the copier delivery team, delivering and installing copy machines. In 1997, I transferred to another location where I resided for two years managing the warehouse, distribution team, administrative staff, lease administration, human resources and building maintenance issues. In 1998 we started our fourth location. I returned to the corporate office in 1999 and started a business leasing company to create an alternative financial option for our customers, as the big leasing companies we had partnered with were becoming less friendly. In 2002, we opened our fifth location and in 2004, I took over the corporate operations. At the end of 2005, I finalized the purchase of the remaining shares of the entire corporation, thus ending a 14 year acquisition process. In 2009 the company employs approximately 300 employees.

Challenge and Vision

Advisor: Shortly after we started the coaching, Carl began to see the importance in not only his development but also how others could join in this process to support the business transformation he began three years prior when he purchased the company from his father. The transformation journey was one of individual leadership transformation for Carl and also organizational transformation for the company. Like traditional business transformations, this included a great deal of complexity but was complicated by the nature of transforming a business that is family owned. One year into the process, we are seeing significant positive results.

As the consultant, my experience of this transition is that all of the participants genuinely wanted what was best for the company and for the family. They were able to stay actively engaged and work toward positive outcome even when their beliefs about what should be done or how it should be done differed. I make this comment about not only the family members but also other members of the senior leadership team.

Carl: When I started working with the Advisor and identified areas of change, there were three succession challenges that I faced: Respect of History, Habit and Culture. "Respect of History" revolved around our top five leaders, who have each been with the company for a minimum 35 years. It is wonderful to draw from such a vast array of experience they bring to the table, however it presented a challenge. How could I respect their contributions to the company but move towards a more competitive business model that conflicted with some of their methodologies? "Habit" was a problem because these managers were used to working directly with my father and not me. Being the new guy on the team (only 17 years with the company), my involvement was often an afterthought to them. I would hear "Oh yeah, has anybody asked Carl about this?"

The third issue was a difference in "Culture." My father's team had molded their actions to my father's expectations, and now I had taken over with a different set of expectations. I was working towards a culture of higher accountability and standardization while his culture was more relaxed and autonomous. His model worked fine, but as we continued to grow and the economy began to weaken, the shortcomings of his culture became apparent to me. One example is that certain managers felt their style was being cramped when I had requested that all locations use the same sales order form, same delivery form, etc. I didn't care who put it together or what it looked like, I just wanted all six locations using the same form. I quickly figured out that getting the paperwork to match was not the real issue, but rather it was getting the managers to accept the benefits of standardization and giving up "control." It took nearly a year before the pushback subsided.

Carl's Process of Creating a Compelling Vision

Advisor: Carl and I initially focused on his personal vision both for himself and for his company. This allowed him to identify where we would go with our work; his vision has served as the foundation for our process. We used a structured approach to defining his vision that involved several exercises directed toward vision along with a series of questions shown in Table 6-1.

The integral nature of the questions lent themselves well to organizational transformation in that they addressed Carl's personal vision in the context of his role as CEO, as well as his role as husband and family member. He took all of these into account when he established his personal vision. Carl completed the exercises on paper and reviewed them with me weekly. He answered all of the questions to enable him to clarify his vision.

After defining his personal vision and starting the organizational transformation process, he first worked with his company's president and then his leadership team to define a company mission and vision.

> **Vision: Consistently supports our client's success by being the best business technology services organization.**
>
> - Serve as trusted advisors providing services that enable our clients to improve their business performance and sustainability;
> - Run a sustainable, profitable business that rewards accountability and results;
> - By promoting client success we continue to build MT's track record of supporting our employees, customers, community and owners.
>
> **Mission: Highly talented people helping our clients succeed by using best practices to deliver consistently exceptional products and services with outstanding technical support**

This process was very iterative and took about 6 months from Carl's initial vision until the leadership team agreed to the wording of the vision and mission. I believe this was influenced in part by the fact that the company had functioned very successfully without a formal mission and vision. The leadership was focused on getting results and this type of discussion was perceived as taking time away from doing the work of running the business.

Introduction to Bruce

Bruce was an MBA student who participated in my Leadership Class at Capital University. He used the Field Book as his textbook and completed the exercises within a 3-month period. As an independent study he revisited his journey a year later, updated his goals and reflected on his results. You will read his words about the process over more than a year of his individual journey.

My name is Bruce, and I am a 40-year old engineer responsible for leading continuous improvement in a large healthcare system. I am married, and have two children. If you had asked me a little while ago if I was a leader, I would have more readily identified myself as an engineer, possibly a teacher, but not a leader. I realize more now that I am a leader, just not the classic type that you tend to read about in books.

Before I get too far, allow me to tell you a little about myself. I grew up on a farm, far from the city, learning to appreciate a simpler way of life. It was here that I gained my love of nature and appreciation for the natural beauty around us. I always had a desire to understand how things work, so becoming an engineer was a natural step. At the same time, I was intrigued by how the human element factored in, so I became an Industrial Engineer, as human-factors are a key part of this discipline.

I have served in the military, involved in leading communications units, and even have some experience overseeing Public Affairs for a large military organization. From there, I moved into manufacturing. While I did well in these settings, I was never truly happy or content, as it felt like something was missing. It took me a while to realize it was a sense of giving back to the community. It was for that reason that I finally moved into healthcare. The very nature of my work was improving the care of the patient. It also allowed me to achieve more balance in my personal life. This is very important to me, as I value my family very highly. I have found over time that this sense of balance is critical to my success.

If you were to ask me where I see myself in my leadership development, I would place myself solidly in the Individualist category. Being strongly introverted, I have often been reflective growing up. However, coming from a small rural setting, and then being an engineer, I wasn't necessarily exposed to a wide range of views and cultures. Over time, I have come to understand that there are many different views and opinions, and I have come to understand that different does not equate to wrong. I realize that others do not see the situation the same way that I do, and that is a good thing. I can learn to understand those differences, see what I can gain from them, and, more importantly, think through how I will communicate my views in a way others can understand.

I wish to share some of my journey as I walk you through my use of the tools outlined in this book. It has helped me a lot in defining the type of leader that I want to be, and helped me develop my plan in achieving the vision for myself. I hope you find it meaningful.

Bruce's Process of Creating a Compelling Vision

In my personal vision, I am living on the family farm down in a rural setting. I do some small farming with a few animals and space for a sizeable garden to grow food. My wife, kids, and I spend time working in the garden, working on projects together, and spending time in nature. We are involved with the community in such items as 4-H and church. My wife and I joint chair a small group or two with our children, such as 4-H, Boy Scouts, or Girl Scouts. I continue to develop my hobby in magic, taking time to do children's sermons at our church and the occasional special message for adults.

I work for a large Midwestern Hospital System helping staff and leadership develop systems for continuous improvement, working to improve the clinical and financial performance of the hospital, allowing it to better serve the community. While I lead some projects, my key role is that of facilitator, developing the staff and leaders to recognize opportunities and implement solutions so they can address day to day issues on their own.

I find both my work and personal life very fulfilling. While there are high demands on both sides, I usually manage to keep a good balance between the two. I feel as if I am able to give back to the community and those around me in both arenas. I run 4 days a week, and try to do some strength training 3 days a week. This combined with the work on the farm helps to keep me in shape and helps to keep my mind more focused.

My Values

The values exercise was challenging, as it forced me to whittle down my personal values to what I have defined as my big three. In so doing, I can then compare the decisions I make in my life to these key values and determine if my decisions are in line with my values.

Top 10 Personal Values	Top 5 Personal Values	Top 4 Personal Values	Top 3 Personal Values
1. Close Relationships	1. Having a Family	1. Having a Family	1. Having a Family
2. Community	2. Integrity	2. Integrity	2. Integrity
3. Competence	3. Nature	3. Nature	3. Nature
4. Growth	4. Helping Other People	4. Helping Other People	
5. Having a Family	5. Involvement		
6. Helping Other People			
7. Integrity			
8. Involvement			
9. Nature			
10. Wisdom			

Family has always been important to me. Growing up, I spent a lot of time with my family, being able to spend time with my parents both at home and in the work they did. I had a lot of respect for my parents, and wanted a family like that for myself. Family is where you can share the deepest part of yourself and know that you will always be accepted, even if they do not approve of what you are doing. It provides a sense of security and grounding for me, and helps to allow me to be more confident in other areas of my life.

Integrity has always been core to me, and without it, nothing else matters. If people are not able to trust you and what you say, you are not able to help them. When they know they can rely on you and what you tell them, they will more readily consider what you have to say and your insight, even if they do not agree with you.

Helping other people and involvement are synonymous for me. You must be involved to help others. There is no way you can do this from a distance. Nature ties in that I realize we are directly dependent upon nature. By taking care of nature and appreciating it, we help ourselves and those around us.

Define Direction

Vocationally, when I look at what I am passionate about, it boils down to helping people. Even though I am an engineer by education, I have also considered teaching, personal coaching, and Christian ministry. However, due to my technical background, and my desire to problem solve, none of quite resonated with me the way that my current role does.

By transitioning to healthcare, I have an opportunity where my day-to-day work can directly benefit members of the hospital and the people in the community. In addition, my role is really that of a mentor, working with different areas of the hospital to understand the issues at hand and helping them to define the corrective plan that is needed. I can honestly say that I look forward to work more now than I ever have in the past.

Financially, I can make a comfortable living in this line of work. I can't live an extravagant life, but I can definitely provide for my basic wants and needs, which is all I really desire. At the same time, I still have plenty of room to grow to develop myself and grow within the organization.

Tell My Story

Reflection: I have known for a while what I would like. I am challenged by where I would like to live. While I love the farm where I grew up, the economy is stifled and my opportunities to find work in the area are extremely limited. This, however, changed when I moved into healthcare. As I continue to gain more experience in healthcare, I see my opportunities to find work down there grow, as I am sure I would be able to find a position with one of the hospitals in the area. It will continue to be a challenge, though, as many of the hospitals are not as forward-thinking as my current employer, yet, and may not see the full need for a strong continuous improvement program.

I have not made the move, yet, because I want to be able to provide a certain level of income/living for my family. This has kept me from looking for lesser opportunities that might currently exist. As I move forward, I will also have to consider my family. My son has been evaluated with autism and ADHD, so as I consider a transition, I will need to be sure that I move to an area with a school system that can accommodate his special needs, a medical practice skilled in his needs, and a support structure for my wife and me.

Self-Image: I am an honest and straight forward person. I say what I mean, and consider honesty to be a highly valued trait. I am willing to have the difficult conversations needed to move a project or the organization forward. My focus is on what is best for the patient or community.

My material wants are small. I would like a farm in which to live and grow food. I don't need the latest car, just something functional to get me where I need to go. My clothes are functional, and can be found at just about any basic department store.

In my ideal living environment, I balance the needs of work and family. When I come home, I am able to put work behind me and focus on my family. My accomplishments outside of work are just as important as my accomplishments at work.

I am physically fit. I keep an eye on my health to make sure that I am generally eating well, working out, and getting plenty of sleep, but I am not obsessed about it.

My relationships are few, but deep. There is very little I am not willing to do for a family member or friend, as long as it is ethical.

Vocationally, I am in a mentor role, helping those around me and the organization move towards their full potential. I am in healthcare, as my accomplishments at work also help to give back to the community. I am not in the spotlight as a leader, but rather, in the background, making sure that everything is in place to work smoothly.

In personal pursuits, I continue to develop my skills in magic and music. I do well in both, but I will never be a master. That is okay, as there are so many other things to do. Travel is occasional, visiting places of either historical or ancestral significance.

My family and I are involved in the community, finding our own unique way to give back to those around us.

Life Purpose: My purpose is to help those around me. My main role is to help others grow and develop. Life is not so much in the doing, as it is in the trying and learning, finding myself just a little bit better than I was the day before. I continue to grow in my ability to connect with those around me and I also grow in my ability to see and understand their unique point of view.

If I could have it all now, would I take it? That is a tough question. Would I like to have it? Absolutely! I'm not sure that I would take it, though. Some items, such as living on the farm, I absolutely would. Other items, such as facilitating a larger group in a hospital, require me to go through a certain amount of growth before I can achieve them. Bypassing that growth does not help me or those I would seek to serve.

In the area of family, I really need to learn more about understanding my family's needs and being there for them. While I have improved in this area, there is still much that I need to do. Providing me additional work responsibilities until I have mastered, or at least improved, this would prove detrimental.

I still need to build up my personal confidence in confronting others. I tend to shy away from conflict, and this is not something I can do when I am trying to lead. I am attempting to improve on this by evaluating what will happen if I do not speak up, but this is still a work in process. Also to help with this, I am working to better understand the counter-point-of-views of those with whom I interact. Only then can I present a constructive argument that is respectful of their opinions.

I am already in a mentor-type role with my current work. It has taken me a while to realize that this is where my strength really lies. I have done various leadership positions within both the Army and manufacturing, but I would never say that I was truly happy or satisfied. Before I moved into healthcare, I was looking to go back to school to be able to teach. My timely move into healthcare has allowed me to balance my skills in operations with my desire to teach and has really been a good fit for me.

Within the past 6 to 8 months, I have worked to improve my general health. I exercise more regularly, and my eating habits have improved, even if they still are not what they should be. My biggest struggle is making sure that I get enough sleep. As I continue to prioritize and eliminate those things from my life that I do not see as valuable, I should find it easier to make time for sleep.

If I would to look for general themes in my vision, one of the first and foremost is that of an educator/mentor. I like to be able to help others and see what they can accomplish. Another important theme is family and my ability to be there for them. Too often, I have given more time to others than I have to my family. This unbalance creates tension and *is not fair to my family. This is a trait I have learned from my parents, and I continue to struggle with it on a daily basis. However, I do at least realize that this unbalance exists, and I can continue to work on it. The final theme is nature. I have a deep love and respect for nature. This is a big reason why I desire to live on a farm. While I may not currently live on a farm, I can do what I can to help nature and allow adequate time to get back to nature and rejuvenate.*

Your Process of Creating a Compelling Vision

Now that you have read the personal narratives of Jill, Bob, Carl, and Bruce, it is time to complete the exercises and answer the questions in Table 6-1 for yourself. We encourage you to complete all of the exercises. This chapter serves as the foundation for your personal vision, values, and course of action so exercise patience and give yourself time to explore your hopes and dreams as authentically as possible. You will know when you've completed this chapter and are ready to move to the next when you feel you have created a vision and set of values that truly inspire you.

Throughout this chapter we have discussed exercises for you to use to create a compelling vision for your own life and work. This process can be a very meaningful one, helping you clarify your life direction. The rest of Section II focuses on the actual process involved to bring your compelling vision into existence.

CHAPTER 7:
Analyze Your Situation and Strengths

Figure 7-1 Innovative Leadership Development Process

Now that you have begun developing more clarity about your vision, we suggest that you also begin to further examine your strengths and development opportunities. This chapter will help you refine and clarify those strengths and weaknesses using standard assessment tools. You will then decide what areas you would like to improve by either building on those you already do well or correcting weaknesses. We recommend employing a general guideline that focuses 80% of your effort toward building your existing strengths and 20% on addressing weaker areas. Though this percentage is a general approximation, it is a directional rule stemming from the belief that you are already successful and have simply taken the opportunity to further advance and refine your capabilities. If you do find yourself experiencing serious deficiencies, you may want to spend more time addressing those using whatever resources you are drawn to beyond the scope of this fieldbook.

It is important to combine your vision with a firm understanding of your current performance, abilities, personality type, and developmental level. This set of data will help you clarify how you see yourself and how others see you. The combination of information will help you determine the gap between your current state (based on assessment data) and your vision.

It is important to note that many people have a higher capacity than they are able to use at work. This could be caused by working in a job that does not use your full abilities. When you begin taking assessments, it will be important to get information from a broad range of sources to ensure you have a clear and accurate picture of your true capacity.

Assessment Tools

One of the primary ways to help you understand your current development and performance is using a combination of assessments to measure your current skills and abilities along with your personality style and developmental level. This should allow you to determine the gap between your present state and the increased expansion of your potential.

Leadership Behaviors

Situational Analysis

Resilience

Developmental Perspective

Leader Type

There are several good assessments available. We have used the suggested tools extensively with our clients and recommend them with a high degree of confidence. Moreover, we find that each tool provides vital information in helping to convey a comprehensive picture of strengths, weaknesses and opportunities. These assessments are aligned with the 5 leadership domains discussed in Section I of the book.

There are many highly reliable and effective tools beyond what we suggest.

The first assessment is focused on Type; our example assessment is the Enneagram.

■ **Leader Type Assessment using the Enneagram.** We recommend using the Enneagram:

...first and foremost to *discover your own personality type* and (where possible) to ascertain the types of those we are interacting with. The Enneagram is used for personal growth, relationships, therapy, or in the business world as an indicator of an individual's primary personality type. As you read in Section I, having an accurate understanding of type can be very helpful. The *Riso-Hudson Enneagram Type Indicator* (version 2.5) provides a reliable, *independently scientifically validated* tool for that purpose. Please remember that discovering your type is only the first step in the process of self-discovery and working with this system. Finding your type is not the final goal but merely the starting place for a fascinating and rewarding journey of self-reflection.

The Enneagram helps you see your own personality dynamics more clearly. Once you are aware of the importance of personality types, you see that your own style will not be equally effective with everyone. Thus, one of the most useful lessons of the Enneagram is how to move from a style of interacting in which others are expected to mold themselves to your way of thinking and values to a more flexible style in which you act from an awareness of the strengths and potential contributions of others. By doing so, you help others become more effective themselves—and as a result, harmony, productivity, and satisfaction are likely to increase." (source: www.enneagraminstitute. com/practical.asp)

- **Developmental Perspective** – Here we recommend using the Maturity Assessment Profile (MAP) to evaluate developmental perspective. Susann Cook-Greuter developed this assessment to describe developmental perspectives as part of her Ph.D. at Harvard University. This is widely considered one of the most rigorously validated, reliable and advanced assessment tools used to evaluate adult leadership development. Participants taking the assessment complete the 36 sentence stems (e.g. When someone needs help…?). The freeform response format allows test takers to provide a wide range of information which provides the scorer ample data required to evaluate varying developmental features along three (3) main lines: cognitive complexity, emotional affect, and behavioral/action logic. Action logic is how people tend to reason and respond to life. It is critical for the test subject to be completely open and honest when taking this assessment in order for the scorer to have sufficient data to provide an accurate score.

Figure 2: Sample Feedback from the MAP

Stage	Distribution of 36 responses by sentence #
Impulsive	-
Opportunist	-
Diplomat	-
Expert	17, 23, 29, 32, 34, 35
Achiever	6, 9, 11, 18, 21, 24, 26, 27
Individual	1, 2, 3, 5, 7, 8, 12, 13, 15, 20, 22, 25, 28, 31, 33
Strategist	10, 14, 19, 30, 36
Magician	5
Ironist	-

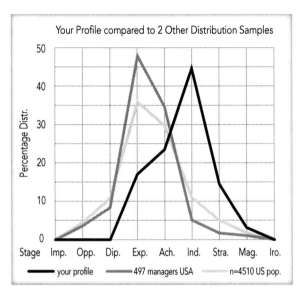

Your Profile compared to 2 Other Distribution Samples

— your profile ▬ 497 managers USA ▬ n=4510 US pop.

- ◼ **Resilience Assessment.** Metcalf & Associates created a basic tool to help you assess your attitudes and practices that help support resilience, and identify those areas where you can further build your capacity. It is based on fundamental stress management research including the characteristics that support "stress hardiness," a concept pioneered by Suzanne Kobasa. In addition, because individuals who function at these later stages are more resilient when dealing with change and adversity, the Resilience Profile includes essential components that are aligned with higher stages in Susann Cook-Greuter's developmental leadership mode. Refer to Part 1, Chapter 3 on Resilience for more extensive details. This assessment is available on the Metcalf & Associates web site.

- ◼ **The Leadership Circle Profile Competency Based 360° assessment.** This tool looks specifically at a set of well-researched leadership behaviors as key levers to drive success. Refer to Chapter 5 in Section I for in-depth information about this assessment.

Figure 7-3 Sample TLCP Feedback

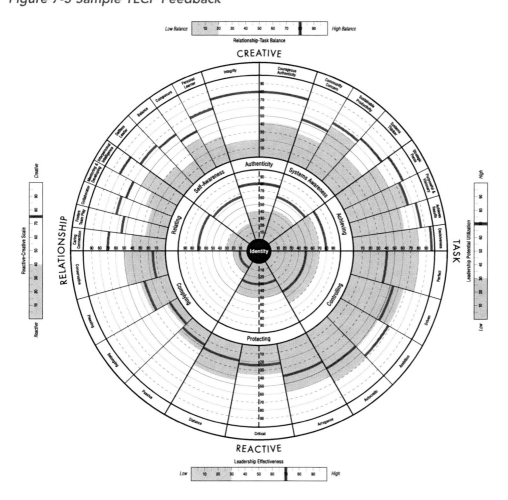

In looking at this simple example of feedback, you will notice that the graph shows high scores in both task creative and task reactive areas (more gray on the right side). From this part of the score we can tell that others perceive this leader as more task focused than people focused. This score may be appropriate for the job or this leader may learn from the assessment that he/she is not giving enough attention to people related components of leadership. An additional piece of information is also important: above the gray shading, you will see a line. This line reflects how the leader self-scored. The leader sees his/her behavior differently than peers see him/her. This difference could be an inaccurate self-perception. It is important for the leader needs to have an accurate view of what others see to be able to make appropriate changes and gauge the impact of these changes. This tool not only allows you to identify possible behavioral changes, it can also help you improve your self-awareness, specifically understanding how others see you. It is this ability to see what others see that will allow you to target your behavioral changes and fine tune your effectiveness.

It is important to note that how others perceive you is, in part, based on their own values and overall view of the world. Interpreting that data can be just as much an art as scientific inference. Rather than taking such feedback at face value, we suggest trying to understand the stance of those evaluations as well as the culture of the organization.

For example, if an individual is very results oriented in a culture that prefers collaboration, that individual may be perceived as having a negative disposition: controlling, driven, and autocratic. Alternatively, another organization with a different culture more aligned with a results-driven approach may perceive that very same individual as being extremely positive: achieves results, vision focused and system oriented. Part of understanding development and effectiveness is finding the organization aligned with your leadership style, as well as a culture that can support the potential to grow.

It is very helpful to take multiple assessments at the same time to paint a more complete and accurate picture of who you are as a leader. For example, the Enneagram shows your personality type; the MAP shows your ability to take multiple perspectives associated with levels of development; and the TLCP shows how you are perceived by others as well as how you see yourself. This combined or integrated assessment allows you to better understand your innate skills and abilities as well as your opportunities. This comprehensive information allows you to determine how you fit within your organization. Keep in mind that interpreting the data from these and other assessments requires specialized expertise and we strongly recommend working with a certified coach. Similar to getting medical tests, the potential value of the information is only realized with properly translation. To that end, having a coach interpret the series of assessments as the foundation for your development plan can significantly increase your results since you will know exactly where to focus your efforts.

Now that we have presented four different types of assessments, you will have the opportunity to select the ones you are moved to take and consider how best to utilize the results. The following examples from my own experience help to convey their practical use:

Example

Client 1's developmental score increased significantly during our two years of working together. Interestingly, however, his 360 score actually declined during that time. We suspect that part of the decline was due to a change in the type of colleagues responding to the assessment the second time. Several employees involved in the second assessment were unwilling to participate the first time because of low trust in the organization. On the surface, the leader could be perceived as less effective during the second assessment. However, the MAP assessment showed a significant increase in scores. The combination of the 2 assessments along with further analysis showed a subjective improvement during a very difficult period for the organization. We also looked at objective organizational measures such as increased revenue and profitability which suggested that, while his 360 scores declined, his leadership ability actually improved. In this case, the assessment was the starting point for further analysis to understand the whole picture. It clearly pointed to the leader's need to address issues of trust with his team.

Client 2 evaluated his entire leadership team. Individuals took the assessment and Metcalf & Associates consolidated the results to reflect the overall team scores. As a whole, the team showed very low effectiveness as compared to the average group of leaders, in some cases in the bottom 10% on a scale of 1-100%. We worked with some of the leaders individually prior to conducting the assessment, and individually they were quite successful. We also worked with one of the leaders after he left the organization and he too was quite successful. What we learned from this specific assessment was that several leaders were <u>less effective in this team</u> than they were in other teams or organizations due more to this particular team's dynamics. Our work together focused on changing the team dynamics as well as helping some individuals address very specific behaviors. In this case, the change involved altering the culture and systems as well as individual behaviors.

In both of these examples we used the assessment tools along with other information to clearly identify the issues and corrective actions. We strongly encourage you to gather data in all four aspects of situational awareness: individual intentions, individual actions, culture and systems. Reflect on your circumstance as well as changes in yourself and the organization. Have conversations with friends, look at your performance appraisals, and examine your company or department performance, including trends and assessment feedback.

The corrective action for these different situations can obviously vary greatly. It is critical to have multiple data points to properly interpret the results. These assessments can function together as a very valuable tool, helping you identify your strengths and weaknesses, and also serve as a data-driven foundation for creating your development plan.

Future Projections

We often find reading futurist publications in specific industries to be very helpful. This information may provide insight into overall societal trends and suggest immanent scenarios that can help you navigate those trends effectively.

There are several organizations providing very effective looks into the future. The role of the futurist is to evaluate current trends and build possible scenarios for how the future might unfold. By building on our capacities for leadership, we can use these scenarios as part of our planning process to ensure we are well prepared for the potential impact of ever-changing business conditions.

One of the organizations we regularly reference for developing trends is the Arlington Institute. At the time of this writing they offer a free newsletter called FuturEdition. The Arlington Institute (TAI) was founded in 1989 by futurist John L. Petersen. It is a non-profit research institute that specializes in thinking about global futures and creating conditions to influence rapid, positive change. They encourage systemic, non-linear approaches to planning and believe that effective thinking about the future is enhanced by applying newly emerging technology. TAI strives to be effective agents of advancement by creating intellectual frameworks & tool-sets for understanding the transition in which we are living.

> TAI believes that in 2009 we are living in an era of global transition, to a degree that our species has never seen before. The exponential increase of human knowledge, and the acceleration of its application through technology, is propelling humanity towards a new era of thought and endeavor. Society, science, ecology and commerce are converging at the intersection of danger and opportunity. A complexity and unpredictability that is beyond our past experience characterize the challenges at hand. If humanity's preferred future is to be realized, new tools for strategic planning and problem solving must be invented and combined. (http://www.arlingtoninstitute.org/tai/mission, 7/25/2011)

Now that we have reviewed the tools for data gathering, it is time to synthesize what you have learned about yourself through a Strengths, Weaknesses, Opportunities and Threats worksheet (SWOT) and through a series of reflection questions. For the SWOT analysis, please complete the following worksheet. For the reflection questions, select 1-3 questions from each of the squares in the table below.

TABLE 7-1: SWOT ANALYSIS

Strengths	Opportunities
What sets you apart from most other people?	What opportunities are open to those who have these strengths?
Weaknesses	**Threats**
What do you need to improve?	Do you have weaknesses that need to be addressed before you can move forward? Do any of these pose an immediate threat such as losing your job?

Innovative Leadership Reflection Questions

To help you develop your action plan, it is time to further clarify your direction using reflection questions. These questions are organized by quadrant to reflect the four native domains introduced in Section I. As a reminder, this is an opportunity to practice innovative leadership but considering how your change plan will affect changes in your intentions, actions, culture and systems. These questions are arranged to help you explore each of these domains. The questions for "What do I think/believe" reflect your intentions. The questions "What do I do?" reflect your actions. The questions "What do we believe?" reflect culture. The questions "How do we do this?" reflect systems. This exercise was designed to help you start practicing innovative leadership as you create your vision and define your direction.

TABLE 7-2: QUESTIONS TO DETERMINE URGENCY FOR CHANGE

What do I think/believe?

- Do you need to change to accomplish your goals? Is the change in perspective or expanded capability at the same level?

- What do you think your developmental perspective is based on how you think and act at work?

- What level do you think is required for you to perform your job effectively now? In the future?

- How satisfied are you with your performance on your goals?

- Are you able to balance business and personal commitments? How is your leadership style impacting your ability to meet your overall life goals?

- Notice your own interpretation of the urgency of the change and what it means for you personally. What will need to change to be the leader you aspire to be?

- How has your leadership style contributed to the organization's success? Have you done things that did not produce the results you had hoped? How would you change to produce different results?

- How would you like to impact the people who work for you? Have they grown and met their career goals while working for you? What have they contributed to the organization while working for you?

- If you are leading a change initiative, what will you need to change to lead this effort effectively? Will you lead the same way this time or will you change from what you have done in the past?

What do I do?

- What assessments are you taking to gather objective data about your performance? This could include performance appraisals, developmental assessments, 360° feedback, or informal feedback from multiple sources.

- How do you model appropriate responses to the sense of urgency in personal actions that are true for you while supporting the organizational objectives?

- What messages do you convey that use emotion, external expert sources, and sense of clarity to demonstrate urgency?

What do we believe?

- Notice the various people and groups in your life and what they report as "urgent." (Family, colleagues, boss, community, friends, etc.) Do people around you think you need to change?

- Anticipate how they will interpret this change. How will they talk about it? Specifically for your business, how will various groups within your organization be impacted by the changes you aspire to make?

- Determine how your sense of urgency connects with the sense of urgency of the group based on their priorities, goals, and pains.

- How does the culture of your support system impact your beliefs about yourself and about leadership? Would these beliefs change if you changed who you spent time with?

- Based on the developmental perspectives, where is the cultural center of gravity in your support system? How are people with more open perspectives perceived? How are people with earlier perspectives perceived? How will this impact your ability to change?

- What are the cultural barriers to you changing? What are the cultural enablers? Will your changes be aligned with the organizational culture? Will they send a message that you do not value the culture?

How do we do this?

- What systems and processes are enablers and barriers that will impact my development?

- What processes and measures alert us to urgency in our system that we need to tend to? What are the early warning signs?

- What processes measure your progress? Are you progressing as measured by criteria that will increase your professional effectiveness? Are you progressing against your personal standards? How will your support system or organization reward or punish your changes based on the measures?

- Do the measures indicate a sense of urgency to you that support your focusing on development?

Analysis by Developmental Perspectives

At the **Expert** perspective, a leader is primarily focused on immediately urgent issues, maintaining and expanding his or her expertise, and focusing on technical skills in areas where he or she is already proficient. To progress toward later developmental views it may be helpful to consider developing skills beyond subject matter expertise. The particular skills to target may be identified from feedback about other areas. This might be considered less important since the previous focus was on increasing functional expertise.

At the **Achiever** perspective, the leader sees urgency in the ability to get things done. If your Achiever capacity is strong, you will likely focus on getting successful results on a project and/or taking on a larger or more complex project or job. You may be concerned with becoming more promotable or becoming more competitive. At this level/perspective, you may be more exhausted and often overcommitted. Achievers would benefit by considering how this behavior is impacts them personally as well as how it impacts others.

At the **Individualist** perspective, the leader's focus is often centered on a sense of longing for more in life; in other words, a feeling that you are not being fully yourself and/or are not living your life's purpose. There may be a sense of urgency in figuring out what that "more" consists of and how to change in order to deal with the gut feeling that you are not doing what you are meant to do. Reflection and noticing what sincerely calls you may be helpful and engaging exercises.

At the **Strategist** perspective, the leader's focus is often on a strong desire to become increasingly authentic and to make a systematic impact in the world by engaging areas he or she is passionate about. During the Individualist stage you began exploring those passions with serious intent, and now you are in a position to effectively engage with people and systems in ways that bring this passion to sustained practical life. Strategists can be highly productive since they are clear about their truest aspirations. Part of your process at this stage may include phasing out or reducing involvement in activities that are not consistent with the intention behind those passions. As a Strategist, you often notice that you are aware of conventional approaches to situations, but are not as constrained by following those conventions compared with your earlier life perspectives.

Stories and Examples

Jill's Responses as a Strategist

To help illustrate what responses to some of these questions look like, we've answered questions from each section for Jill as a Strategist. We took this approach to give additional insight into one possible scenario showing how a Strategist would answer the questions. We also understand that while Strategists can develop the ability to think in terms of multiple scenarios and concrete execution of 15-20 year time horizons, as well as being more aware of their emotional content, they also differ widely in their skills, life experiences, scope and scale of intention, and life passions. Jill provides just one example.

JILL'S SWOT WORKSHEET ANSWERS	
Strengths What sets you apart from most other people? ▬ Strong self-knowledge ▬ I am good at my work and I love what I do	**Opportunities** What opportunities are open to those who have these strengths? ▬ Run a larger organization that makes a greater impact on the world ▬ Teach, mentor and develop others ▬ Continue to act responsibly in the world in all situations
Weaknesses What do you need to improve? ▬ Enhance my knowledge in my field because it is continually changing ▬ Frustration with others who are low performers or cannot see the big picture ▬ Level of frustration ▬ Ability to reframe situations to see the positive or opportunity ▬ The desire for life to work out smoothly and even easily	**Threats** Do you have weaknesses that need to be addressed before you can move forward? Do any of these pose an immediate threat to you such as losing your job? ▬ No immediate threats but certainly areas I would like to improve ▬ Building additional emotional calm and the ability to put challenges into a longer term perspective will help ▬ Realizing that many of the frustrations in life are important lessons for myself and others and that in some cases I just need to let others move at their own pace

Jill's Reflection Responses

What do I think/believe?

- *Do you think your developmental perspective is based on how you think and act at work?*

   I have now tested at "Level 5" or Strategist using the MAP. I am interested in my score because it gives me insight into what I should focus on to build my development plan. I tend to want to "invest" in my development in ways that will make a big impact. I believe the assessment is accurate because I find myself making important decisions based on strong data in conjunction with internal beliefs. I realize that others do not see the world in the same way I do and my decisions are not aligned with "conventional wisdom" at times. In addition to being a "strategist" on the MAP assessment, I am also a type 3 on the Enneagram (the achiever). I have been working with the Enneagram assessment and the MAP for several years to help me sort out what is core to my personality vs. what is aligned with my developmental level. I find that these distinctions can be confusing, and yet as I get a better handle on what all of this data means, I am better able to clarify where to focus my development activities.

- *What level do you think is required for you to perform your job effectively now? In the future?*

   I think I can perform the job very effectively at the Strategist viewpoint. Parts of the job require different perspectives; some tasks require me to function as an expert, others achiever. There are also parts that I can do more effectively because I have the capacity to function as a Strategist. I am able to see the big picture for most issues and also understand the process and tactical requirements. I understand what needs to happen to get results and I also understand how to connect strategy to actions so we are getting the "right" results. In addition to being a strong thinker and analyzer, I have a pretty firm grasp of my emotions. I tend to be pretty calm and people are comfortable coming to me with challenging news. I pride myself in being a calming presence when others show inappropriate levels of frustration in ways that are unproductive in the work place.

While my life is very good, I still aspire to have a broader impact. The more I grow and develop, the greater my impact. This definitely includes a balance of enhancing skills – while I am quite competent in my work, I still have much to learn. Growth is particularly important to me because I believe the world we live in is dealing with major challenges, and effective leadership will help us navigate these issues in ways that will reduce the pain of many people.

■ *How satisfied are you with your performance?*

I am satisfied that I do a good job. I read a great deal so I have the knowledge required. Still, I am learning that this is not enough. I have spent most of my life getting "smarter," Now I need to shift 80% of my focus on becoming more "emotionally smart" and still spend 20% of my time keeping up with trends and changes. This has been really interesting because I did not learn about emotional intelligence until recently and was a bit skeptical about the content really applying to me. I have come to believe that I have some catching up to do in this area. I used the competence/resilience assessment to give me additional insight into where to focus on emotional intelligence. I am getting a clearer picture as I go along about why this matters, and how I can develop to increase me leadership effectiveness.

What do I do?

■ *How do you communicate your personal changes and your sense of urgency to those around you who may be impacted?*

I communicate what is urgent largely by how I choose to spend my time and money. My time is very precious to me so I spend it in ways that will make an impact on what I value like leadership development, sustainability, and the environment. As a result, my volunteer activities have moved from getting involved in several organizations with different missions, which provides a great emotional connection but little actual change, to participating on a Board of Directors for a land preservation organization. My friends and colleagues see how much time and energy I spend on this organization and how I model my own beliefs

■ *What messages do you convey that use emotion, external expert sources and sense of clarity to demonstrate urgency?*

I talk about what I learned on the assessment and what I am doing about it. I also ask others for constructive feedback on a regular basis. I realize as a leader this is a tough question and I want others to see that I am willing to make personal changes to become more effective. When I ask them to do the same thing, they will know that I am asking them to do what I am doing.

What do we believe?

■ *How does the culture of your organization impact your beliefs about leadership? Would these beliefs change if you changed organizations?*

Since I am a Partner in the organization, I have helped shape our culture. We value personal development and individual growth highly in the same ways that I do. This can have pros and cons as we focus a great deal on developing ourselves and model the behaviors in our business working with different types of clients. Not everyone is interested in growth and development, and yet they may still be very competent performers.

I joined a consulting firm because it focused on leadership and organizational sustainability. I value the global fate of people and other living beings on the planet, and wanted to use my years of experience to make the world a better place for the next generation. Because my beliefs are fairly well established, I was very careful to select a company that had similar values. I think I would really struggle in working for an organization that did not value sustainability or growth. I would say this was not true earlier in my career and it was easier to change jobs and be happy then.

How do we do this?

- *What systems and processes are enablers or barriers that will impact my development?*

  Our organization offers the MAP assessment and development program as part of our performance management process for senior leaders, as well as the TLCP 360 assessment for all organizational leaders. We take the MAP assessment every 3 years and the TLCP every 2 years and while we are not required to share our scores, our leadership team evaluates one another and we expect to see improvement. We believe that the organization is only as successful as our leadership so this is a great enabler to drive me forward. For the 360 assessment, we encourage leaders to use the results as the beginning of a dialogue between the leader and his/her team to discuss how they can work together more effectively as a unit. This discussion happens at all levels within organizations.

- *What processes and measures alert us to urgency in our system that we need to tend to? What are the early warning signs?*

  An important measure of success and failure is how well our company is able to make the ongoing changes to scale, both quickly and profitably. If we are meeting client needs, growing our capacity and operating profitably, it is a strong indication that we are functioning well as leaders. If any of these measures slip, we look at the processes and also look at our own behaviors and decisions as leaders to see what we need to do to address the issues. We start with the assumption that we as leaders are responsible for the organization's success and failure, and who we are as leaders has a significant impact both our success and failures. Years ago I was introduced to the Malcolm Baldrige assessment to evaluate organizational success and still find this to be the most comprehensive organizational/leader effectiveness tool. While we do not do a full blown assessment, we do consider the key elements when looking at how we are performing.

Bob's Case Study

Bob took the MAP and tested at Achiever with even distribution between answers for Expert and Achiever. Some of his strengths include a passion for serving people, a strong business acumen, a strong interest in improving the community, and a focus on accomplishing the organization's mission. His biggest area of development is releasing control of the smaller details in favor of focusing on the big picture.

Bob took The Leadership Circle Profile and identified specific leadership competencies that he wanted to refine. These competencies corresponded with those referenced in the MAP. He succeeded by controlling activities through detailed management and significant involvement in details rather than through purposeful and visionary activity and systematic thinking.

Bob: *The assessments were a real eye opener. I was not surprised by some of the assessment results, both positive and negative. Others were more unexpected yet if I looked closely, I could see that the negative attributes did show up in the problems that continued to frustrate me. It is easy to blame others when heads butt and deadlines collapse, but ultimately the desired organization change would come from me, as I changed. With this baseline, I could create a plan with the coach on what to work on.*

Carl's Case Study

Advisor: The assessment process involved both Carl as an individual as well as MT. We started with an assessment of Carl's leadership using the Mature Adult Profile (MAP) created by Susann Cook Greuter and the 360° assessment of leadership behaviors using The Leadership Circle Profile (TLCP). Carl tested as post conventional on the MAP and had many leadership strengths to build on along with some areas for improvement. Part of the assessment process involved sorting out what the scores actually meant. Carl has many strengths that were not leveraged by MT as a conventional organization. Adding to that complexity is the fact that Carl is the son of a highly respected and well-liked leader. The assessment results were used to help identify where he could make the biggest impact with his change efforts.

Along with the assessments, he also continued the quadrant questions exercises tailored to self-assessment and completed a Strengths, Weaknesses, Opportunities and Strengths (SWOT) assessment.

Carl answered the questions in the quadrants and other questions to create a clear picture of his current strengths and weaknesses. At this point, he had clarity around his personal direction and capabilities and was ready to create a development plan.

The organizational assessment activities took place after Carl's individual assessment process. The timing varied as he engaged people in phases, so it has taken much of the year to evaluate key leaders and create their development plans. In addition to leadership assessments, we looked at several areas of organizational effectiveness.

During this phase, one of the key activities was working with Carl and his company President, John H., to define the guiding principles which serve as the initial roadmap for change in culture and processes. We used a series of 20 continua that describe many of the key factors associated with culture.

An example was that each of the 5 locations were highly decentralized and operated as separate businesses with different processes. While that model worked very well to get MT to its current level, moving toward a model with more consistent processes and shared services located at corporate would reduce cost, increase process efficiency, and reduce the risk associated with turnover and unplanned absences. This change required a shift in culture, systems, processes, and staffing levels at the locations.

This is one example of a guiding principle that drove concrete actions in the initial work plan. The template we used is included below:

Centralization

How should resources be organized and located in terms of the business being supported?

We conducted other types of assessments as we went through the process. Some of the assessments were rather informal based on input from both Carl and John H.

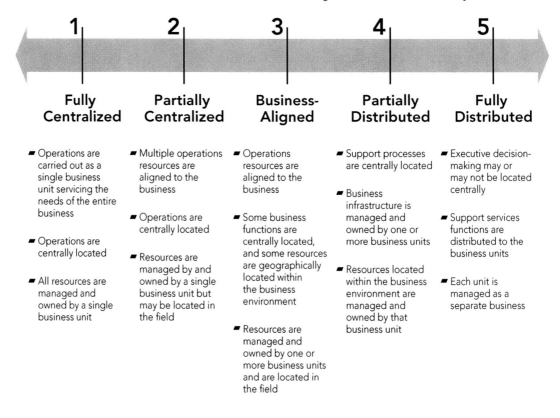

1	2	3	4	5
Fully Centralized	**Partially Centralized**	**Business-Aligned**	**Partially Distributed**	**Fully Distributed**
■ Operations are carried out as a single business unit servicing the needs of the entire business ■ Operations are centrally located ■ All resources are managed and owned by a single business unit	■ Multiple operations resources are aligned to the business ■ Operations are centrally located ■ Resources are managed by and owned by a single business unit but may be located in the field	■ Operations resources are aligned to the business ■ Some business functions are centrally located, and some resources are geographically located within the business environment ■ Resources are managed and owned by one or more business units and are located in the field	■ Support processes are centrally located ■ Business infrastructure is managed and owned by one or more business units ■ Resources located within the business environment are managed and owned by that business unit	■ Executive decision-making may or may not be located centrally ■ Support services functions are distributed to the business units ■ Each unit is managed as a separate business

while others were more standardized including the MAP and The Leadership Circle Profile.

One other significant project we started during this time was a succession assessment. We wanted to understand which key roles were covered and what training was required to develop the next level of leadership. We also launched a financial wellness check up to consider how the accounting and finance function was positioned to support the business as the complexity increased with the expanding corporate strategy.

Carl: *The great thing about the "Guiding Principles" assessment was that John and I took it independently from each other, yet our responses were closely aligned. This meant we had* cleared the first hurdle of not being on the same page. Secondly, it started the process of getting our thoughts on paper. Sure, they have been rattling around our heads for years, but that was of little use when the team could not read our thoughts and everyone was headed in a different strategic direction. Since our management team had historically operated in a reactionary mode, these exercises were viewed as "spending unnecessary resources that did not provide any real value other than to pad the pockets of the consultants who provided them." They believed we were creating more bureaucracy and wasting their time when they could be out selling instead! I saw things differently and felt that we had become inefficient and had lost accountability to ourselves. Sure, we were busy, but not as effective as we could be. It was similar to the old saying, "Selling without profit is like eating soup with a fork. You stay busy, but in the end you starve." I came to realize that this process was not exciting for the people who would rather spend their time in drama-land, but I became really tired of cleaning up messes caused by poor planning or lousy processes. I was no longer entertained by the Superman role of saving the day, and I wanted to get it right the first time in order to spare the excitement.

Before this process, I did not believe that the senior management team was aligned with our strategic direction. Up until 2009, we had always been in a double digit growth mode. And when you are growing, it often feels like you are doing your best just to keep up. 2009 was the first year we had flat growth and our management team started to see the value in this process. Since we could not make money by selling more, we would have to make our money by spending less. This meant that future profits were hidden in the inefficiencies. Suddenly they were more willing to listen to any ideas that would drive down expenses, which eventually put more money in their pockets. Now they were more willing to accept a change in culture. Given the choice, profit through process standardization, project management, budgeting and forecasting, leadership development and strategic planning was more enticing than perceived control through autonomy.

Bruce's Case Study

Bruce: *Up to this point, my entries have reflected where I stood a year ago when I first* *began my leadership journey. Since then, I have been promoted to a senior position within my department, with increased responsibility for defining the direction of our department, as well as a more active role in the organization as a whole.*

I am actively involved in an initiative to improve the operational effectiveness of the organization as a whole, taking a key role in helping to define the process as we move forward. Along these lines, I was assigned one of the key departments that started the whole initiative, due to a combination of my ability to lead larger teams and achieve results, as well as my ability to step into ambiguous situations and get to the root of the matter and help define a direction moving forward. Since working with that team, I have been assigned a lead facilitator role with four other teams, with impact that reaches into all parts of the organization.

On a personal level, I am more involved with my church, taking a role in a small part of the church leadership, while leading some of the children's sermons and participating in the choir. There is more that I would like to do, but I limit myself so that I still have time to complete my MBA and devote time for my family.

Family is the one area I have not advanced myself as much as I would like. While I make sure to guard my family time, there is much going on with my work and spending time with my son and daughter that I do not dedicate as much time for my wife as I should. In addition, due to my strong leanings towards introversion, I find myself very drained at the end of the work day, so I have to work more on my strategies to make sure that I maintain sufficient energy levels when I am home with my family. Diet and exercise help with this, but family requires more of a dedicated commitment than I have done up to the point, at least to achieve what I desire in a family life. This will be a key area of focus in my meditations in the weeks and months ahead.

Your Process of Evaluating your Situation and Strengths

Now that you have followed Jill's descriptions, and the case study responses from Bob, Carl and Bruce, it is time to complete the worksheets. Based on your assessment results, complete the SWOT analysis (Table 7-1) and answer the questions in Table 7-2 for yourself. By internalizing your strengths as well as opportunities you can focus on your proficiencies. Alternatively, understanding your weaknesses will help you know what to avoid, what to improve, and what personal feedback to request from people skilled in those areas. Again, as a rule of thumb, we focus about 80% of our development activities on areas that inspire us and about 20% on areas we must address to move forward.

We encourage you to complete all of the exercises. This chapter helps you clarify your strengths and weaknesses as a foundation for your personal transformation journey. Take your time and give proper attention to gathering input from several different sources. When you have a clear picture of your strengths and opportunities from several different perspectives you will sense that you are ready to move to the next chapter. You may now find that you have a different or clearer perception about where you excel, and how those areas can complement your vision.

In this chapter we have explored a number of tools and questions to use as you continue shaping a compelling vision for both your personal and professional life. Bear in mind that you are creating your own story through this process. The remainder of Section II focuses on the framework to create and implement a development plan that will allow you to close the gap between your vision and where you are today.

CHAPTER 8:
Plan Your Journey

Figure 8-1 Innovative Leadership Development Process

When you plan your journey, you begin investing your development time and energy based on your vision, your strengths and weaknesses, and the actions required to close the gap. In order to stay motivated, it is important to experience a sense of measurable growth. Tangible results are especially crucial to implementing change, and demonstrating progress is naturally part of the expectation. An example is: If my boss wants me to show that I am a good leader before he will promote me, I need to show that I am "good" as measured by the boss's criteria. So, in this case, I would want to understand what the boss values, and build a plan that allows me to show those results. On the other hand, if I am developing for my own personal growth, I may not be as concerned about showing results to others, but I will still want to feel like I am making progress.

As you can imagine, some of the results you are working for will take much longer than others. Our experience with clients has shown that leaders can certainly make quick progress in some areas, while others, such as moving to a later developmental level, will take 2-6 years on average.

Developmental advancement will also be impacted depending on your life situation. For example, a leader with an Achiever perspective may be a great provider for his family, and this is a core value he holds. Thus, he may not experience a shift in developmental perspective during this time because his needs center heavily on career and money. Even so, he can still create meaningful results that help cultivate developmental growth. In other words, he may simply experience a sense of progress ranging from a greater feeling of calm, clearer thinking, and better relationships with colleagues. He may also see measured results quantitatively, using a 360° assessment showing significant improvements in key leadership-related qualities.

Additionally, consider the value of investing your energy in this journey as a way to foster meaningful change for the people closest to you. If you know, for example, that you have specific behaviors that are particularly difficult for your boss, an important colleague, or a loved one, you may want to prioritize those areas for improvement.

Options for Focus of Development Plan

To accomplish your vision, you may benefit from one or all of the following:

- **Becoming more effective at your current developmental perspective** – Changing behaviors that will significantly impact performance, as measured by performance evaluations and 360° feedback.

- **Advancement in developmental level/perspective** – Developing in a way that is tested by the MAP assessment; also called *vertical development*. This means more than changing behavior; it entails a shift in how you relate with both the world and yourself. For example, a shift from being the best at your craft to being the one who makes plans several years into the future in order to accomplish your goals. You would retain the excellence in your craft; but now, perhaps, at far less expense of achieving completion of tasks.

- **Building on your current strengths** – Development can take the form of focusing on enhancing current strengths. It can also focus on important behaviors that adversely impact success. We recommend focusing 80% of your effort on building on your passions and 20% of your effort on shoring up your deficiencies. While this is a rule of thumb, it is important to remember that your specific situation and needs will be a clear indicator of what changes are required for your continued growth and success.

- **Minimizing your weaknesses** – In the Strengths, Weaknesses, Opportunities, and Threats (SWOT) analysis, you may have identified some behaviors that you need to correct, having determined that they may likely impede further growth. These may have been behaviors that made you successful in your current development (sometimes referred to as *overdone strengths*); even so, part of your development is examining the events and behaviors that got you here and those that may interfere with your success at a higher level position within the organization. For example, you may identify yourself as someone who is on top of every task. As your team and responsibilities grow, you will delegate more, but you may still feel uncomfortable with your lack of knowledge of the details. Trying to manage the details to the level that made you successful will become a weakness as you move up. It is important to tend to these behavioral changes as part of your plan. So, the challenge here may be shifting the focus and expanding your ability beyond one or a few core strengths to develop several additional capabilities.

As you begin building your capacity, you may want to consider two distinct yet essential areas. Research among Fortune 500 companies at Stanford University showed that 90% of those who failed as leaders did so because they lacked the interpersonal skills that are a critical component of emotional intelligence. This is confirmed by research conducted by the Center for Creative Leadership that shows that poor interpersonal skills are a leading cause of derailment from executive-level positions. While this research is compelling, most of our formal training focuses on hard skills. This exclusive emphasis on hard skills leaves many leaders ill-prepared and in some cases uninformed about the importance of this internal capacity.

- ◢ **Internal capacity:** This includes intention, worldview, purpose, vision, values, cultural norms, emotional stability, resilience, a sense of being grounded, overall personal well-being, intuition, balanced perspective, and attitude. Internal capacity serves as the foundation for you to accomplish your deepest aspirations. Additionally, this internal capacity is required to move on to later stages of development. Cindy Wigglesworth's research on developmental levels hypothesizes that you cannot fully sustain the individualist perspective until you demonstrate enough emotional intelligence, and you can only consistently embody the strategist perspective after you embody appropriate spiritual perspective. Practices like meditation are very helpful in enhancing these attributes.

- ◢ **External capacity (hard skills)** – These are skills and behaviors associated with professional success; this is where most professional development efforts have been placed.

In most organizations, the vast majority of development efforts focus on hard skills (including advanced degrees and certification programs), and thus many leaders need to balance them by explicitly exercising internal capacity. To further describe this process, we use the term *mastery*, which simply means the capacity to not only produce results but also to master the principles underlying those results. In other words, as a master, you can deliver results with a level of comfort from the internal capacity behind your skills and judgment.

Personal mastery involves enhancing your internal capacity to support the skills you have acquired to the best of their ability while also removing barriers to your success. To help you achieve personal mastery, we recommend you enrich your ongoing development plan and personal practices (activities we repeat until we master them, like our golf swing).

There are some important factors to consider when creating your plan. First, you will get more leverage if you cross-train or develop several areas at the same time. According to Ken Wilber in his conversation on the **AQAL Framework DVD**, there are benefits to cross-training beyond simply focusing on one area. For example, people who both lift weights and meditate tend to make greater improvements in both areas than those who do one or the other. Evidence suggests that a combination of activities from different parts of our lives complement one another, and this is quite true in the leadership arena as well.

A comprehensive plan will take into consideration each of the following dimensions that are foundational to human experience: physical, emotional, mental, and spiritual (or for people not comfortable with the term *spirit,* altruistic or intuitive could be substituted). If any of these elements are neglected, you are likely to find that it will adversely impact your success in other areas over the long term. There are standard programs designed to help this process.

One of the programs we like is Integral Transformative Practice (ITP) developed by Michael Murphy and George Leonard. This practice involves a strong cross-training routine. The system's nine commitments form the essential building blocks of the ITP program. They create the roadmap for practitioners to follow to realize their potential through the cross-training of body, mind, heart, and soul. The commitments include aerobic exercise, mindful eating, strength training, staying emotionally current, a service component, and the ITP Kata, which is a 40-minute series involving movements derived from yoga and Aikido, deep relaxation techniques, imagery, affirmations, and meditation. ITP is a long-term program for realizing the potential of body (exercise), mind (reading, discussion), heart (staying emotionally current, community), and soul (meditation, affirmations). If you are interested, you may find an ITP group in your area that will augment a strong individual practice.

Tools and Exercises

The range of tools is quite broad; therefore, it is important to select something that feels safe and consistent with your values. The goal is to create a plan that you can follow and stick with to accomplish your goals. To help you get started, we put suggestions into the categories in Tables 8-1 and 8-2. While there are several items that may fall within multiple categories, we tried to classify them to be as mutually exclusive as possible. Growth includes vertical development practices (progressing through developmental perspectives), horizontal practices (getting more effective at the current developmental perspective), and activities and that will help both types, such as meditation.

Healthy development encompasses work in all areas. The practices you choose may change, and your practice may also fluctuate based on other life demands. We do encourage you to maintain as much consistency as possible. Just as the benefit of exercise increases when you hit a specific frequency and duration, the same will be true for leadership development practices. The more you invest, the better your results will be.

TABLE 8-1: RECOMMENDATIONS FOR INTERNAL AND EXTERNAL CAPACITY BUILDING - ACTIVITIES TO CONSIDER INCORPORATING INTO PLAN

What activities can I do to impact my internal capacity (what I think and believe)?

- Spirit
  - Define vision
  - Define values
  - Meditate
  - Pray
  - Participate in religious practices
  - Religious study
  - Seek spiritual counseling
  - Seek a spiritual teacher
  - Visualize
- Ethics
  - Create guiding principles or values

- Ethics
  - Create guiding principles or values

- Emotions (Emotional Quotient)
  - Meditate
  - Seek therapy
  - Practice HeartMath techniques – see resources for more information
  - Practice shadow exercises
  - Keep a journal
  - Seek coaching
  - Maintain strong friendships

What activities can I do to impact my external capacity?

- Body
- Exercise
  - Yoga
  - Relaxation
  - Lift weights
  - Mindful eating / healthy diet
  - Sufficient sleep
  - Mindfulness-based stress reduction
- Mind
  - Read
  - Study
  - Attend lectures and discussion groups
  - Attend school
  - Perspective-taking exercises
  - Take stretch assignments
  - Volunteer for opportunities to build skills (charity work)

- Ethics
  - Become socially active – volunteer
  - Pay attention to ethics around you

- Cross Training
  - Integral Transformative Practice (yoga, aikido, relaxation, visualization, meditation)
  - Reflection practices (do-reflect-learn)

What activities can I do that impact us as a group (what we think/believe)?

- Review the list above, and determine which activities can be completed in a group. What groups do I participate in, and do they have similar values?
- You may find that, as a family, you develop a mission and values. You may choose to set family meditation time or gym time to promote a family sense of focus and wellbeing. Many families share religious traditions and find that they provide a solid foundation and a shared set of values.

What structures and/or groups will help? What groups or programs do I participate in?

- Family activities could include how we eat, our exercise routines, our family reading time, our church or spiritual practice, and our volunteer activities.
- Friend/social activities include what I do with my friends that supports and that hinders my development, such as exercise groups, emotional support, honest and accurate feedback, and dialogue practices.
- Work events and support, including yoga classes, weight management support, fitness classes, insurance discounts for fitness, and smoking cessation programs
- Practice groups for development, such as Integral Transformative Practice, meditation, and church
- Study groups
- Formal education programs
- Informal education programs
- Fitness groups and programs, such as running clubs, ski clubs, exercise groups, and gym memberships

Following is a partial list of recommendations that may be helpful for vertical development, as measured by the MAP assessment.

TABLE 8-2: RECOMMENDATIONS FOR VERTICAL DEVELOPMENT (MOVING TO THE NEXT PERSPECTIVE) – ACTIVITIES TO CONSIDER INCORPORATING INTO YOUR PLAN	
Perspective	**Development Recommendation**
Diplomat *(Focused on maintaining status quo and not making changes to the system)*	- Direct, supportive mentoring (can be parental) - New responsibilities and skill training - Gratitude practice - Assertiveness training - Public recognition for initiative-taking - Learning incentives and awards - Institutional membership - College degree to broaden and deepen skills, build critical thinking and judgment
Expert *(Focused on improving and accomplishing tasks)*	- Mentor/coaching by someone at one of the later developmental perspectives (Achiever, Individualist, etc.) - Mindfulness-based stress reduction or yoga - Gratitude practice, keeping a journal, meditation - Clear goals and objectives with specific measures and feedback mechanisms - Time management and decision tools - Attend training programs like "management by objectives", delegation, or "Managing People for Results" - Reward for results and for accomplishing strategic priorities on time and within budget - Management and budgetary responsibilities - Listening and interpersonal skill training - Participate in a multidisciplinary program, such as an MBA (not a program that develops additional expertise in a single discipline) - College degree to broaden and deepen skills, build critical thinking and judgment

Perspective	Development Recommendation
Achiever *(Focused on achieving desired outcomes in a way consistent with self-chosen values)*	- Mentoring/coaching by Strategist - Mindfulness-based stress reduction or yoga - Reflection practice, meditation, gratitude practice, keeping a journal - Practice Action Inquiry techniques, ladder of inference, dialogue; uncover assumptions and blind spots (see Fifth Discipline Field Book and Action Inquiry) - Practice Noticing exercises: Pay attention to assumptions, feelings, and behaviors that would otherwise pass you by. This will generally be after the fact; allow time for these exercises - Transfer learning from other disciplines. Expand perspective about how other parts of the organization, other organizations, and other industries operate - Pay attention to how unique individual circumstances and needs impact your ability to accomplish goals. How do these factors impact others' abilities to accomplish goals? - Review and refine career goals and direction through trusting and probing conversations about what the leader values, with the intent of expanding their perspective to focus on larger and broader goals - Participate in program focused on developing integral approaches that put equal emphasis on the interior dimensions of both individual and collective development (intention, worldview, purpose, vision, values, and cultural norms) and on its exterior, or visible, dimensions (behaviors, organizational structures and processes), and how shifts or interventions in these domains must be coherent for change to be both deep and sustainable
Individualist *(Creates opportunities to have meaningful and satisfying experiences that support sustained achievement of goals)*	- Mentoring/coaching by Strategist or Magician/Alchemist - Self-care – eating, sleeping, mindful eating - Mindfulness-based stress reduction or yoga - Reflection practice, meditation, gratitude practice, keeping a journal - Practice collaborative inquiry (group exploration and questioning, such as dialogue) and reframing to understand projects, alliances, and organizations; and explore what the group requires to become more successful - Strengthen network of peers who can and will challenge your assumptions and help you expand your thinking

Perspective	Development Recommendation
Individualist *(Creates opportunities to have meaningful and satisfying experiences that support sustained achievement of goals)*	- Increase self-motivated, self-generated learning - Expand noticing – cultivate an awareness of your body, feelings, and thoughts in the present. Expand this ability beyond times of meditation; practice it during daily activities. - Broaden involvement in multiple areas of action (personal, social, economic, civil, and professional) and networks - Deepen awareness through therapy, ongoing dialogue groups, keeping a journal, hobbies, and physical and spiritual practices - Expand self through creative and artistic expression - Create alone time every day for a meditative practice to enhance your attention and self-awareness (options range from shamanic drumming to traditional Christian centering prayer). - Develop awareness of multiple voices within self – this can be accomplished with voice dialogue technique or therapy. Practice listening to guidance from the spiritual voice or still, small voice. Strengthen connection to still small voice. - Practice both/and thinking which is a movement beyond seeing situations as either this or that. Practice seeing both this and that. Explore polarities. - Notice limitations of consensus and involvement - Clarify life purpose, and focus energies on making a contribution to that purpose - Identify how your life is connected to others. Identify who you want to serve and how – this could be a sense of responsibility for your family and community. At later stages, who we serve seems to expand to broader groups - Participate in program focused on developing integral approaches that put equal emphasis on the interior dimensions of both individual and collective development (intention, worldview, purpose, vision, values, and cultural norms) and on its exterior, or visible, dimensions (behaviors, organizational structures and processes), and how shifts or interventions in these domains must be coherent for change to be both deep and sustainable

Perspective	Development Recommendation
Strategist *(Experiences the fullness of life; is of benefit to self and others)*	■ Working with a Magician/Alchemist coach – use inquiry process to see that whatever they judge or perceive as outside of themselves may also be true about themselves (the nature of projection). We also encourage them to witness the moment, breathing and feeling their bodies to connect with their feelings, hearts, and vulnerabilities; and when they are truly ready to move into construct awareness, we encourage them to begin to consider letting themselves feel what it is like to let go into the unknown. (Source: PI paper in ILR 4/11) ■ Seek coaching that supports seeing that beliefs are constructs when there is a natural readiness for this. (source: PI Paper in ILR 4/11) ■ Self-care – eating, sleeping, mindful eating ■ Mindfulness-based stress reduction or yoga ■ Consider adding daily or weekly review of life purpose and top 3 goals. At this stage, goals will likely include acting in alignment with your values, such as being compassionate in all interactions. ■ Work through psychological issues, and become aware of limitations (source: Barret Brown PhD dissertation) ■ Expand noticing practices, shadow work, meditation, keeping a journal, gratitude practice, or reflection exercises ■ Become aware that experiences are a result of an event and that our story or meaning is us making ties with that event/situation; be aware that we are creating our own meaning ■ Strengthen spiritual practice to connect with power beyond self on a regular basis – listen to that small still voice ■ Continue to cultivate connection to still small voice, and allow that voice to have a greater role in decision making for large and small decisions ■ Notice how your actions impact others and the interconnected nature of all beings. Examples: Where do toxic chemicals go when we dispose of them? When we are kind to someone, how does that positive action ripple through the community? ■ When you perceive others as harming or frustrating you, take the opportunity to see the situation from their eyes (shadow work and perspective taking). If you change your point of view based on this exercise, reach out and reconnect with the other person to discuss your new awareness ■ Practice looking at situations from multiple perspectives. This is what I see from where I sit – how would someone else see it?

Perspective	Development Recommendation
Strategist *(Continued)*	• Practice centering exercises in the midst of uncertainty – be aware of desire for quick fix vs. ability to allow situations to unfold
	• Continue to seek feedback from trusted others
	• Continue to take action toward fulfilling life purpose – be aware of daily activities and which ones feel life giving vs. life draining
	• Participate in program focused on developing integral approaches that put equal emphasis on the interior dimensions of both individual and collective development (intention, worldview, purpose, vision, values, and cultural norms) and on its exterior or visible dimensions (behaviors, organizational structures and processes), and how shifts or interventions in these domains must be coherent for change to be both deep and sustainable
	• Develop awareness of presence of ego and how/when it is impacting action. Connect more deeply to presence, and release constructs of the ego
	• Practice Big Mind meditation – see Gempo Roche or other forms of voice dialogue

The following is a Development Plan Template designed to help you create a plan that allows you achieve your goals. This table focuses mainly on identifying opportunities and the intentions behind your desire to change. It is a good tool to use in conjunction with a 360 degree feedback tool.

TABLE 8-3: HORIZONTAL DEVELOPMENT WORKSHEET
Evaluate and Select Behavioral Change Priorities – Worksheet

Key Actions	Key Actions	Horizontal Skill 1	Horizontal Skill 2
Select Behaviors	Which behaviors do I want to improve or change? Which behaviors do I perform well that I would like to enhance?		
What are the consequences of this behavior?	What will happen if I continue to demonstrate this behavior in the future? How will my customers be impacted? How will my career be impacted? How will my colleagues be impacted? How will my organization be impacted?		
Why do I demonstrate this behavior?	I have developed behaviors over the course of my life because they make sense. What has changed to now make this behavior ineffective?		
How would I like to perform in the future?	Write an end-result statement describing the changes I will make and the impact of those changes. What will an observer see when I have made this change?		
Who will help me change?	Who could I ask to provide me with feedback on how I am doing? Who could be a good mentor?		
What type of support do I want?	Make an agreement with a person you trust about how you would like to support one another in changing behaviors. How will that person hold me accountable for taking this step? How will I support them in changing their behavior? Is there a group that will support me long term?		
What will I do or not do?	What other actions could I take? What am I willing to commit to doing? What am I committed to stopping?		
When will I complete actions?	When will I have completed action items?		

The next template was designed to synthesize development activities reflected in the prior worksheets focused on horizontal, vertical, and cross training.

We recommend that all goals be SMART as defined by the following:

- **Specific** - A specific goal has a much greater chance of being accomplished than a general goal.

- **Measurable** - Establish concrete criteria for measuring progress toward the attainment of each goal you set.

- **Attainable** - When you identify goals that are most important to you, you begin to figure out ways you can make them come true. You develop the attitudes, abilities, skills, and financial capacity to reach them. You begin seeing previously overlooked opportunities to bring yourself closer to the achievement of your goals.

- **Realistic** - To be realistic, a goal must represent an objective toward which you are both *willing* and *able* to work towards. A goal can be both high and realistic; you are the only one who can decide the height of your goal; but be sure that every goal represents substantial progress.

- **Timely** - A goal should be grounded within an approximate time frame. Goals lacking time frames also lack urgency.

Using the information from all of the worksheets and templates provided, you are now ready to complete your Development Planning Worksheet. This worksheet should reflect the synthesis of your data gathering and personal reflection. This will serve as the foundation for the actions you will take to accomplish your goals.

TABLE 8-4: DEVELOPMENT PLANNING WORKSHEET
Development Planning Worksheet

Current State	Future State / Goal	Actions	By When?	Measure - How do you know?

Innovative Leadership Reflection Questions

To help you develop your action plan, it is time to further clarify your direction using reflection questions. These questions are organized by quadrant to reflect the four native domains introduced in Section I. As a reminder, this is an opportunity to practice innovative leadership by considering how your change plan will affect changes in your intentions, actions, culture, and systems. These questions are arranged to help you explore each of these domains. The questions for "What do I think/believe?" reflect your intentions. The questions "What do I do?" reflect your actions. The questions "What do we believe?" reflect culture. The questions "How do we do this?" reflect systems. Thus, we designed this exercise to help you start practicing innovative leadership as you create your vision and define your direction.

TABLE 8-5: QUESTIONS TO GUIDE THE LEADER AND ORGANIZATION

What do I think/believe?

- What are my priorities for development? Are they reflected in the plan I created?
- Am I willing to make the changes necessary to meet my goals?
- What do I consider personal short-term wins?
- What wins do I want to see in what time- frame? Is this reasonable?
- What do I consider a win for my team?
- What do I consider a win for the organization?
- Which short-term wins will be really important to key people in my life?
- How do I keep motivated to work toward goals that will take a long time or a lifetime to accomplish? How will I think about life changes, such as changing eating habits vs. dieting?
- Have I taken into account the whole range of activities I need to create a sustainable change, such as involving others and creating a plan that I can live with long term?

What do I do?

- How do I translate my vision into long and short-term goals?
- Are your goals SMART?
- What are my financial goals and milestones?
- Is this a plan that is sustainable long term? Will accomplishing my short-term wins motivate me to keep on track with my long-term plan?
- Does my plan contain the foundation work as well as skill building (example: basic health as well as business competencies)?
- Which wins can I identify and support that solve problems that are seeds for future shifts?
- Which changes in my behavior will demonstrate a strong statement to others and encourage their ongoing support while also possibly modeling changes that could also serve them?

What do we believe?

- Which wins will provide meaningful tangible and emotional results, and gain support of key stakeholders in my life?
- Which wins will encourage others to engage in their own personal/professional growth initiatives?
- Which stories can we tell others about the wins that were shared with the organization to encourage them to focus on their development?
- Which wins are reinforced by the culture and values? Which wins would be opposed to our culture and values?

> **How do we do this?**
>
> - How do I align my goals and short-term wins with the organization such that I receive support for the changes I am making? How do I ensure that early wins are important to key stakeholders?
> - How do I track and measure my wins and their impact against overall personal and organizational goals? Do I have early warning measures?
> - Are my wins aligned with the larger organizational objectives?
> - Does the organization reinforce and reward the behavioral changes I am making?
> - How will I connect my personal wins to the organizational vision and measures to demonstrate the impact of my small steps forward?

Analysis by Developmental Perspectives

Leaders with an **Expert** perspective are likely to want to focus on developing additional expertise in their field with developing interest in emotional capacity and reflection skills. For most people, the idea of building additional expertise in their field is attractive. Depending on your level of specialization, you may want to expand your focus and build new softer skills that will complement your strong job-related skills at which you already excel.

Leaders with **an Achiever** perspective may have overtly focused on development to better meet goals. If you are acting from this perspective, you may be less oriented toward developing inner capacity and more focused on developing skills and abilities, and increasing speed so you can produce both more and quicker results. You will also have a higher level of agility in working with direct reports than the Expert leader.

Leaders with an **Individualist** perspective will likely include greater focus on learning more about others, expanding their capacity to build alliances and networks, as well as influence through others. When you take this perspective, you will also be paying more attention to getting in touch with your inner processes through tools that foster self-reflection. For many people, this is a very new activity, and they discover an entirely new way of experiencing themselves. Moreover, according to Cindy Wigglesworth's research, she hypothesizes that for leaders to successfully embody the Individualist perspective; they must develop and consistently apply enough emotional intelligence. For those who are already strong in this area, they may not need to focus as many resources on this area; but for most leaders, this won't take priority until at least the late Achiever stage.

Leaders with a **Strategist** perspective are able to balance the needs for building alliances, tending to processes, and delivering results. According to Cindy Wigglesworth's research, to fully embody this perspective, the leader will have some spiritual or altruistic perspective or intelligence (this is different than religion – it is an orientation toward something bigger than themselves and their organizations). This can be summarized briefly as having a sense of a world far greater than the individual. They also tend to develop a sense that they have a great deal of mastery over our own reaction to the world, so they experience a greater sense of balance in their interactions. Because Strategists generally have a strong reflective practice, they have a stronger ability to disconnect from daily dramas, and they can put their lives into perspective. For Strategists, a tough interaction can be just that: it is tough, but it does not need to be blown out of proportion. For this reason, it becomes easier to maintain that sense of balance for longer periods of time.

Stories and Examples

To help illustrate these developmental responses, we've answered questions from each section for Jill as a Strategist.

Sample Responses for Jill as a Strategist

Following are Jill's responses, including her sample development plan and reflection questions. At the Strategist perspective, she is focusing on a broad range of skills and considering her development with its influence on her ability to impact her legacy across the many people and organizations she is involved with.

JILL'S DEVELOPMENT PLANNING WORKSHEET – JILL EXAMPLE

Current State	Future State/ Goal	Actions	By When?	Measure – How do you know?
Assess current developmental perspective by completing MAP and test at Strategist. I would like to develop further as well as enhance my current capacity.	Increase effectiveness. Become more adept at seeing multiple perspectives and comfortable with allowing results to emerge rather than controlling Enhance inquiry skills	1. Perspective-taking activity – using action inquiry 2. Meditation 3. Action inquiry focused on response to ambiguity	Focus on these actions for the following year.	Greater internal capacity - more perspectives leads to greater consciousness. Re-assess using MAP and benchmarking current results.
Assessed physical and emotional health through metrics, such as weight, exercise habits, emotional resiliency, etc.; and I have work to do	Become more emotionally centered and healthier physically.	4. Meditation 5. Exercise regularly 6. Mindful eating	Focus on these actions for the next 6 months.	Increased sense of overall well-being and comfort in own skin. Re-assess using previous metrics.
Business successful. Compile financial statistics.	Grow business as indicated by specific metrics identified in the current state analysis.	7. Identify potential marketing/PR firms 8. Write a recurring column in a national magazine focusing on organizational transformation	Focus on these actions for the next six months	Improved profitability and brand recognition. Re-assess using previous metrics.

Jill's Reflection Responses

What do I think/believe?

- *Are my goals SMART?*

I used the worksheets provided, and my goals now fit the criteria of SMART. It took me a few tries, but I am now getting more comfortable with what I am trying to accomplish. I tend to feel more comfortable setting my direction using my vision and guiding principles; and yet I still find value in creating clear goals. I know I will continue to refine them as I go, and they are good enough to start. An example is I will make time every day for self-care, like meditation and working out. I may also do walking meditation so I can get some exercise while I am meditating and reflecting. I am not willing to take a job that requires me to work more than 60 hours per week.

- *What do I consider personal short-term wins?*

In the short term, I am focused on understanding what is important to as many of our stakeholders as possible (perspective taking). Given the amount of transition in our world and more specifically with the need for innovative leadership, I am finding that things I took for granted are changing rather rapidly. For that reason, I really feel the need to find ways to appear confident so the people who work for me can focus on their jobs rather than worry about what will happen next. I will continue to use meditation and grounding techniques and a solid work-out regimen to promote this sense of calm. This is both a short-term and long-term goal. I do not see it as something I will accomplish only once, but rather I will need to maintain this long term. This will require that I change how I look at taking care of myself, as I have tended to just put my head down and work more when the pressure rises, then I can get burned out. I have always been overly goal focused, and now I see that the only way I will be able to maintain my balance long term is to take time every day to take care of myself.

- *Which wins do I want to see in what time-frame? Is this reasonable?*

In the next 3 months, I would like to develop the habit of using practices I noted in my goals, like action inquiry so I can do a better job of dealing with ambiguity. While I have practiced action inquiry for years, I am now setting clearer goals for most of my meetings and activities, and I am evaluating how I am doing either on an ongoing basis or shortly after the meeting. This process generally only takes a few minutes, and it really helps me be more productive in each interaction. It also helps me regain focus when things go wrong. The quicker I can correct missteps, the shorter the time I spend revisiting situations that did not play out as I wanted.

I already have a meditation practice and spiritual study practice. I will continue these, and I will track how I am feeling on a mood check list (simple 1-5 score each day). In addition, I am trying to reduce my need to control the world around me and feel more spontaneous. I would like to feel more comfortable when plans change and a greater ability to accept the many chances life has presented me that I never would have imagined or chosen. Some of these changes have become great blessings, and yet I really resisted them. This means remembering that I can relax and allow others to shine, and I can focus on what I can and should control.

What do I do?

- *Have I created a plan that will allow me to accomplish my short-term wins? Is this a plan that is sustainable long term? Will accomplishing my short-term wins motivate me to keep on track with my long-term plan?*

  I believe my plan is sustainable in the long term. I also believe I will not accomplish my goals if I do not take these or similar actions.

  I hope that accomplishing my short-term goals will help me stay motivated. I have found in the past that short-term success can seem good enough so I stop or take a break from my goals. Since this is a lifetime journey, I know I will need to sustain my efforts, while also acknowledging that just moving in the same general direction as my plan may be fine at times. I also need to accept that I will take breaks in my progress.

- *How do I incorporate specific tangible goals into the timelines?*

  I have developed a series of daily and weekly practices that serve as a structure to move me consistently toward my vision and goals – with reflection activities on a regular basis. While I vary in my adherence to these practices, I continue to return to them when I get a sense that I am off track.

On the business side, we have a business plan and standard targets and measures. As a Partner in the organization, I use standard and well-proven business tools to establish and track our progress, such as a balanced scorecard.

■ *Am I willing to take the actions required to generate these wins?*

I believe I am willing to take the actions necessary to succeed. As I think about my personal growth, I am finding that what motivates me to continue has changed a great deal. I am currently heavily focused on what my work will bring to the world. I continue to think about how at one time I worked very hard to move to the next level; I realize I am now more motivated by the impact I am making on others and on the world. While I still want to succeed, my definition of success is broader – it is more about the organization than about me personally.

What do we believe?

■ *Which wins will provide meaningful business results; gain support of key stakeholders in my life?*

I hope people notice that I am calm and peaceful most of the time, and I hope that they trust me enough to raise issues quickly. I hope that I am more productive in meetings because I am focused on what is going on rather than being frustrated by what happened earlier in the day or worried about what will happen next. I expect these changes will be subtle but noticeable.

How do we do this?

■ *How do I align my goals with the organization so I will receive support for the changes I am making? How do I ensure that early wins are important to key stakeholders?*

I was fortunate to find a company that shares my values. The Partners talk frequently, and we are all focused on our personal growth along with organizational success. They see how my development supports the business and vice versa.

- *Does the organization reinforce and reward the behavioral changes I am making?*

I am fortunate that they do support the changes. Specifically, we are facing significant organizational pressure every day, and my behavior directly impacts the ability of our employees to meet customer needs. Additionally, I am making tough decisions that change on a daily basis. I need to have a clear head and emotional balance to work in this type of pressure. With world conditions fluctuating significantly, we do not know whether our clients will continue with their projects, and that will impact our Venture funding. We are at an important and volatile phase of our business in all areas, and my performance is critical to our success. This will be measured by standard business and financial measures, as well as employee retention and leadership team feedback.

Bob's Case Study

Create an action plan that clarifies goals and tactics. The client developed a plan of action for personal and professional growth. The primary focus was to create a plan that supported overall personal and organizational success, then implement timelines on those initiatives. He created an initial action plan, and then modified it over time to reflect his progress and changing organizational situation. The plan included:

Personal short-term goals:

- Improve communication—react to difficult situations constructively;
- Improve stamina—exercise regularly;
- Increase emotional resilience—meditate and journal regularly; and
- Reconnect with family and friends—list friends and family members, and actively connect with them on a regular basis.

Bob: It is one thing to say that I have a problem with listening; it is quite another to gain an understanding of what is involved in effective listening. The advisor was able to provide both a fundamental, state-of-the-science education on the ideal process, as well as a means to enact the desired new behaviors. And she kept me honest. When I relayed the challenges I continued to encounter, she could bring me back to seeing how this related to my spotty listening, etc.

Organizational change short-term goals:

- Develop dashboards on a quarterly basis, reporting financials and performance against goals established by the board;
- Update process flow charts and job descriptions;
- Determine back-ups, and cross train for key processes;
- Update policies and procedures;
- Update document management plan and processes; and
- Gain IT support for key projects.

Bob: I'll admit that I resisted letting go of my death grip on every little detail. The irony was that as I spent less time obsessing over the next item in my task list and invested more time in planning, it was actually liberating. On the personal side, I had believed that in order to meet the demands of the job, I had to sacrifice the things that I used to do for myself. But actually, the more I thought about what I loved in my life, the more I realized that those things reinforced the best in me. I also realized how much they crossed over. My passion for my work was reinvigorated when I began to see it once again as a way to express myself as a good man doing good in the world. The more true I could be to myself, the more I could develop what I love about who I am, the more I had to offer everyone: my family, my community, and my work. The work that I was doing with the coach to create the foundations of a better organization, created an environment that was more manageable. More manageable was less threatening and allowed for more thoughtful and less reactive leadership.

Carl's Case Study

Advisor: Carl's development plan was significantly influenced by his goals for MT. His plan involved working on and in the business. In addition, he continues to maintain his involvement in other organizations, such as Young Presidents Organization (YPO). He remains very committed to work and family balance and he has a strong health-oriented regimen that includes regular exercise, triathlons, healthy diet, and regular sleep habits. He also has a strong marriage with a wife who encourages him to maintain his focus on himself as a whole person. His goals were to move to the next developmental perspective and also to develop additional business acumen.

Our individual leadership development work focused on his setting intentions, taking action, and reflecting on his results as well as his approach. We worked together closely during this time. This process was based on the principles laid out in the book *Action Inquiry* by Torbert & Associates. The plan involved establishing weekly sessions where we would work together and implement changes within the company and discuss how effective the changes and the leadership behaviors were in accomplishing goals.

> Action inquiry works primarily from the inside-out (although it recognizes the presence and influence of outside-in perspectives as well). Action inquiry begins because we (any one of us, or any family, or organization) experience some sort of gap between what we wish to do and what we are able to do. The awareness of this gap can lead to the development of a clear intent to accomplish something beyond our own current capacity. In such a case, the very intent to act includes two elements: (1) the intent to do the inquiry necessary to learn how to do this new thing and (2) the inquiry necessary to learn whether we really have accomplished it. So, action inquiry begins with inner experiences of gaps and intents.

> "If our intent is clear and strong, we will wish to learn the truth as soon as possible about whether our strategies, tactics (e.g., our use of the hammer), and outcomes are accomplishing the intent or not. If our intent has not been accomplished, the sooner we learn this, the sooner we may correct the course of action in order to move closer to our intent. From this point of view, a method that can correct error in the midst of ongoing action is qualitatively more useful to us, more beneficial for others, and more powerful in a scientific sense than methods that *alternate* action and inquiry. Action inquiry *interweaves* research and practice in the present." (Action Inquiry by Torbert & Associates.)

Carl: I would guess that many people perceive that leadership development is achieved by reading another business book or attending more seminars. My experience is that leadership development is about changing the way you think, which determines how you view the world. It isn't necessarily about knowledge or data, it's but about perception and process. For me, it was about the interconnectedness between our customers, our employees, the marketplace, and the economy; not just about selling copiers, but about who were we to the marketplace – how MT fit into the big picture. We would examine how great leaders viewed the world, and we compared that to my thought process. My perceptions and positions would be challenged again and again, but I grew tremendously from the experience, and still continue to do so. Again, I was occasionally criticized because we spent time understanding how I thought rather than doing more "organizationally visible" things, such as creating another new process. Golly, I was sure spending a lot of money on consultants just to "sit there and yap."

Advisor: On the organizational side, the initial plan was shaped by the guiding principle assessment. From the 20 continua and the gaps between current and goal state in each, we identified the actions that needed to take place to close the gaps. We created a scorecard to define and track these actions. The order and timing were driven mainly by the priorities of the business. The following is a small excerpt from the scorecard that was used for the first year to plan and monitor the organizational transformation process. This addressed the culture and the system and process changes.

Goal	Measure	Status	Performance against goals
Run existing business profitably and sustainably	Progress against stated targets – define reports to serve as key and leading indicators	Green	▪ Complete turnaround of x business unit ▪ Maintain profitability in all locations (Controller to meet with GMs to track progress against goals and against benchmarks) ▪ Determine where to integrate IT services into the existing business to better serve current clients and leverage the entire sales force ▪ Maintain customer satisfaction – deliver against customer expectations ▪ Expand client base

| Define mission, vision, strategy and guiding principles | Complete with full support and commitment of leadership team | Green | • Confirmed mission and vision with leadership team - done
• Set clear business goals – x revenue and x% profit margin by year/by location – will become activity of leadership team
• Set employee and community goals – X profit sharing (based on revenue and profit) and community donations of x (based on revenue and profit target)
• Share guiding principles with leadership team – will become part of leadership training
• Define activities required to accomplish key goals and operate company according to the guiding principles (many already in process and included on this document) |

Carl: *The Scorecard is basically our corporate "To Do This Year" list. We use it as a high level communication device, so everyone clearly understands where we are to focus our efforts. It identifies our specific goals, how we measure success or failure, gives a current status indicator (red, yellow, or green), and provides specific and measurable tasks.*

This may appear to be similar to project management, but it is not at the granular level PM is. If done correctly, the items in PM are prioritized according to the initiatives on the Scorecard list. Our company just began using project management two and half years ago. This year, we created a project management office. This was essential because we had 49 projects and no central point of organization. Initially, project management was not well received because our culture perceived it to be cumbersome and bureaucratic. In the beginning, PM seemed very time consuming, since we had to learn the processes and enter the data. Things began to smooth out after our third meeting, (one per month), as we were becoming familiar with the process. Today it provides a great structure for our management team to view how we are prioritizing projects and utilizing resources. It also puts an end to associates being pulled from one job to another without completing anything.

Bruce's Case Study

While I have not achieved everything that I desire professionally, yet, my focus in the coming months will be to maintain what I have accomplished up to this point, and make some small incremental improvements. In keeping in line with my values and vision, my focus will be on my family goals. I truly want to improve my current relationship with my wife, so I will be working on strategies and communications with her to increase our time together doing activities that are valued by both of us. This will result in a better state of balance for both of us, and will improve my effectiveness in all areas of my life.

Professionally, I will be solidifying my current work, while working to position myself for higher levels of responsibility within the department and organization. While there is still much I can do at my current level, I realize that there is more I can do for the organization in a larger role. I have the basic tools to be successful, but I need to improve my skills from both a technical/professional level, as well as from a personal interaction and work relationship level. Only in improving in these areas can I better serve my organization and the community.

Your Process of Creating Your Development Plan

This chapter provides a great deal of information from which to create your plan. Keep in mind that it is easy to create a plan that is too ambitious or complex. We encourage you to commit to small changes you can complete, and then update your plan after you have accomplished your initial goals. Please remember our rule of thumb: try to focus about 80% of your development activities on areas that inspire you and about 20% on areas you'll need to improve upon to help move you forward. The rest of Section II focuses on implementing your development plan.

If you have not done so already, it is time to complete the worksheets and answer the questions for yourself. We encourage you to complete all of the exercises. This chapter serves to help you clarify your action plan, and will help to close the gap between where you are today compared with your newly defined vision. This plan will greatly enhance your efforts toward actualizing where you want to be, as well as making a positive impact on the world.

CHAPTER 9:

Build Your Team and Communicate

Figure 9-1 Innovative Leadership Development Process

In this chapter, you will begin to identify the individuals you want to support your personal and professional development, and the specific roles you envision them playing during this transition. After selecting these people, you will consider the best ways to communicate your needs and receive their feedback. Here, you will carefully choose individuals you feel will be most supportive of your growth. This is both a vote for who is involved in your development and who is not. Your selection criteria should include: experience and skills in areas you want to develop, level of unconditional personal support, ability to offer constructive and valuable feedback, capacity to support transformation, and professional support and advocacy.

You will benefit from choosing a diverse, yet trusted set of individuals to support your development. This is particularly beneficial if you plan to make changes that significantly impact them as well. These individuals can come from various areas of your life, both personal and professional, and can have differing levels of involvement. Some, for example, could be fairly causal, such as a co-worker who is willing to give you feedback after a meeting about a specific behavior you may be experimenting with as part of a new growth plan. On the other end of the spectrum, you could arrange a more methodical, long-term agreement like a formal mentor or coach. You will also want to consider the role your spouse or partner plays if you are part of a couple. Anyone involved must agree to give you honest and supportive feedback. The common thread for all individuals you ultimately invite to share in your journey is a firm trust and belief that, above all else, their support is unquestionably in the interest and service of your growth and success.

As another option, your development support could be found within a team setting. For example, if your goal is to run a marathon your development support could come from a range of options. It could be as simple as joining a running group to support a fitness goal such as training for a marathon. You might also select very specific individual running partners. Other options could include finding expertise from third-party sources such as running magazines or finding on-line groups that discuss tips and progress. You may even select a group where the explicit purpose is to strongly hold each other more accountable.

Professional development can be supported in similar ways. Many organizations are in place to support professional change. These range from coaching and training firms to companies that focus on helping you improve your presentation skills. Depending on your needs, your individual selection of development support may have components of some or all of these choices. Some of your support may be focused on hard skills while others take on a more supportive role like a coach.

After you have selected your support team, the next step will be deciding on methods for each individual to communicate authentic feedback. This is the stage where you ask others for specific kinds of support, including possible behavioral changes on their part. As a leader, you will be letting people around you know that you are engaged in a process of ambitious personal growth. Because people often create a sense of personal safety by being able to predict how others around them behave, it is important to inform your closest circles that you are taking on a structured change process that may involve behaviors they are likely unfamiliar with. The key message here should convey that this process will take time and you will use these new behaviors with varying levels of effectiveness until you master them.

While the information you share will change over time, the need for communication is critical throughout your development process. Communication will happen with different groups of people at various times, and will likely take on different tones depending on the audience and degree of impact. Some people will simply need to understand that overall change is underway. You will want others to make significant contributions to support your behavioral change. What you communicate and when will depend on your relationship with the individual or group, and the type of support you are asking for.

During your process, you may also be asking others to change. For example, in the workplace, you may be communicating information beyond just the scope of work in order to help your staff, coworkers, associates, employees and direct reports develop stronger business acumen. Moreover, you may want others to change their overall style of communication with you. As you model these new behaviors, be aware that some of your colleagues will change quite naturally while others will require more specific and formal discussions to adjust to this new way of relating. As another example, you may want to delegate more and possibly different tasks as well as giving people more freedom to determine how they accomplish assigned tasks. In this case, you could open a dialogue explaining that you are trusting them to determine the most effective approach and will be available to offer support if additional input is needed. Though many employees would perhaps respond favorably to the openness, some will likely be confused if you are not explicit with what you are trying to accomplish.

Support Team Selection Criteria

Providing support to someone who is committed to a process of personal growth is an honor and a tremendous responsibility. It is important to select a development team judiciously since you are, in many ways, requesting these individuals to be trusted advisors.

The following is a rough list of key competencies and selection factors for you to consider. This is a starting point when creating your own selection criteria:

Performance: Consider selecting people who have mastered concepts, skills or behaviors that you would like to develop in yourself. Performance could be as simple as that person having expertise in your field, or a field you want to explore. He or she could have strong interpersonal skills and empathy, or have hard skills such as financial analysis that you would like to enhance in yourself. These individuals could also be people you respect in general. If you are focused on developing advanced leadership skills, you could certainly benefit with mentoring and support from someone you believe is successful against these measures.

Coaching or Therapy: Depending on your development goals, these skills can certainly be helpful.. In some cases you may find that both are valuable. If you are inclined toward developing your developmental level/perspective, you may also want to evaluate the developmental level of the coach or therapist as this can be an important factor in the support they provide.

Personal or Family Connection is important in balancing your development and professional focus with your family commitments. They could be siblings, a partner, spouse or another close friend that feels like family. Ideally, they would help you maintain a balanced perspective of your life based on a historical connection as a whole rather than just the immediate view that a new coach or therapist may have if you haven't worked with them long.

Willingness and ability to commit time to your development are imperative. It is certainly helpful to ask those committed to supporting your development how best to optimize your time together and also discuss your mutual needs. The idea is that everyone should benefit from a clear understanding of how to both support the growth process and create healthy reciprocity. Keep in mind that there are many very well-meaning people who would love to help but realistically are overcommitted, and would not be able to provide the type of support you are looking for. There are others who may lack strong support skills, like the ability to give open and honest feedback. It will also be important to consider the time commitment you desire. Be willing to explore options that allow you to minimize the time you request. You may consider creative options like volunteering for a board that your mentor or support person is on. This would allow you to learn directly and also support that person in meeting their objectives at the same time.

Tools

The following worksheets are designed to help you connect your development action plan with the people who will help you accomplish these goals. They will fulfill different roles ranging from encouragement and support to providing skilled expertise. You may also choose to include those who may be more directly impacted by the changes you are making. The more information and input you can provide during the process, the more likely they will be to support you or communicate their concerns to help you re-align your goals. For an example of the completed worksheet, see Jill's answers later in this chapter.

TABLE 9-1: SUPPORT TEAM WORKSHEET
Support Team Worksheet

Goal	Type of Support I Need	Role	Skills/ Knowledge or Other Criteria	Arrangement
		▪		
		▪		
		▪		
		▪		
		▪		
		▪		

Once you determine your support team and their corresponding roles, you will want to figure out communication, timing and expectations. This is the place to consider the kind of feedback you might expect from others to ensure you are making meaningful progress. This communication can provide you with invaluable information and feedback that is critical for your success. Since your plan is based on your own intuitive senses, the ongoing data should confirm your assumptions, serving as a feedback mechanism to refine your thinking.

TABLE 9-2: COMMUNICATION PLANNING WORKSHEET				
Who	What to Communicate	What They Can Expect from You	What You Want from Them	How Often

Innovative Leadership Reflection Questions

To help you develop your action plan, it is time to further clarify your direction using reflection questions. These questions are organized by quadrant to reflect the four native domains introduced in Section I. As a reminder, this is an opportunity to practice innovative leadership by considering how your change plan will affect changes in your intentions, actions, culture and systems. The questions are arranged to help you explore each of these domains. The questions for "What do I think/believe?" reflect your intentions. The "What do I do?" questions reflect your actions. The "What do we believe?" questions reflect culture. The "How do we do this?" questions reflect systems. This exercise is designed to help you practice innovative leadership as you create your vision and define your direction.

TABLE 9-3: QUESTIONS TO GUIDE THE LEADER AND ORGANIZATION

What do I think/ believe?

- What qualities do I want in the people I ask to support my personal change?

- What qualities will I eliminate from my current and future team?

- How do I think my change will impact those close to me?

- Will my change help those close to me become more successful according to their definition of success?

- Why would others spend their time and energy helping me develop?

- How much support do I expect from others?

- Am I making reasonable requests of those close to me?

- Am I looking for others in business or professional groups who are making similar changes?

- Do I want people around me to change along with me?

- Do I need to improve my communication skills to improve my ability to seek support for my growth? Do I understand that my effectiveness at communicating to others as well as listening to their feedback hinges on my ability to communicate effectively?

- Because my development may be a very personal and often private choice, what am I willing to communicate to others?

- How do I think my preference for privacy or sharing will impact others' responses to my changes and their ability to do what they need to do to either support me or accomplish their jobs? Do I solicit their input and support? If so, how and when?

- What personal stories (actions and emotions) will convey my commitment to my personal change in a heartfelt manner while also empowering others to act?

- Do I need to communicate anything to the organization or just to my support group?

What do I do?

- Who do I ask to participate in my change?

- How do I determine and communicate the criteria for the right people to support me? "Right" includes personality traits, innate capabilities, skills and knowledge, and time and willingness.

- Once I know the criteria, who are the right people and how do I figure out what roles I would like them to take in support of my success? How do I invite them to support this important personal transformation?

- Who do I need to support my development for it to be successful? How can my personal development activities or successes help these key people meet their personal objectives?

- Who may become a barrier to my change? How do I mitigate their negative impact? What are immediate steps and longer term action steps?

- What commitments and actions should I take that demonstrate my belief that change is possible?

- How do I "walk the talk" and show my conviction through my actions? Am I making the changes I say I will? Am I asking for input and acting on the recommendations others give me? If I do not take their recommendations, do I explain why?

- How do I ask for feedback? Am I clear about what information would be helpful to me and what information would not be helpful?

- How do I communicate my struggles appropriately when I fall short of my stated goals along the way

- How do I deliver messages tailored to different supporters that motivate them to continue to help me accomplish my goals?

- Can I be a role model for others during my change process to encourage them to expand their own capabilities?

- How do I convey messages that will make strong statements using the languages of both feelings and of logic to appeal to each individual supporter?

- How do I demonstrate humility and genuinely appreciate the support others are providing?

- How do I communicate my personal vision in a manner that is hard hitting and realistic and still conveys my confidence that I can achieve it with their support?

- How do I communicate progress, new challenges and my commitment to what I am doing?

- How do I communicate the facts and my hopes for the future?

- How do I communicate that the balance between challenge and overload is important and I want to maintain balance as I move toward meeting my personal vision?

- How do I communicate my need and desire for accurate feedback?

- What do I communicate when my situation and priorities change?

What do we believe?

- What are the social and cultural norms that dictate what type of support I should ask for and expect?

- How do we use my personal change as an opportunity to test new behaviors and demonstrate their positive impact on the group (professional organization, family, community)?

- Do the current social and cultural norms still fit for where I am/we are going?

- Do I have the right support to change the culture of our group to allow me to sustain the changes I am trying to make?

- What are our beliefs about who does the communicating? How much information do they share? How often? Do we solicit input or just convey information?

- What is the appropriate language and message content based on the values, goals, language, and culture of each audience segment (organization, family, community)?

- What type of feedback will I seek from supporters to determine if they are supportive of my personal changes? This may be objective and/or subjective?

- Does our current organizational culture and approach to communicating support me in making the changes I am trying to make?

How do we do this?

- What are the key skills and behaviors that support my transformation are necessary in my team? What are the gaps between my current support team and the team needed to support transformation? Do I have the right people available with the right skills and behaviors? Do I need to augment my support team with professionals such as a coach, therapist, spiritual advisor, clergy, colleague or boss?

- What is the best combination of approaches for me to meet my support needs? Does this include hiring a coach or scheduling regular lunches with a trusted colleague?

- What trust building activities can we conduct to improve my sense of comfort with those supporting me?

- What personal and professional metrics should I track to understand if I am seeking and receiving the appropriate level of support?

- If the transformation is a long one, how do I acknowledge the support others are providing? What happens if someone I thought would be a good supporter does not work out, such as a colleague changing jobs or moving out of the area)?

- Am I communicating what supporters believe is important to them? Do they see the progress they hope to see?

- How do I communicate wins to stakeholders to sustain their reinforcement and energy?

- What is my communication approach and plan? Who wants information? When? Through what medium? What are the key messages? How do I keep multiple supporters informed with the right amount of information at the right time to enhance buy-in and support my behavioral change?

- Do we have any applicable stories connected with group folklore? (Remember the time xxx did xxx – guess what happened to me this week)

- Can we combine and/or eliminate any current communications? Are we talking about things that are not supportive of the change I want to make?

- Would communication be more effective if my changes were discussed in conjunction with other topics that either impact or are impacted by my change? Maybe as a group, we are trying to change and we can talk about our progress or about personal and organizational changes and how they are linked and impacting one another?

- How do we communicate measures and rewards for successfully accomplishing our behavioral changes? How do these changes allow us to be more effective as a group?
- What communications are we currently providing that should stop because they are not consistent with the changes we are trying to make?
- How do we measure the impact our communication has in supporting our change?
- How do we improve our communication based on what we are learning from our conversations?

Analysis of Developmental Perspectives

The Expert leadership perspective tends to focus on building expertise. It is likely that leaders coming from this vantage point will be looking for a support team with expertise in the area they aspire to develop. They expect communication to focus on facts and to inform. Experts tend to ask for input from people they perceive to be experts in their field. They will place lower value on emotional intelligence and some of the softer skills than they do hard skills and expertise.

Leaders with **Achiever** perspective tend to focus on success and are likely to find people who will complement their skills or help them develop skills to achieve results, career advancement or public recognition. Their communications may tend to be relatively short and more direct with to less focus on emotional nuance. Time spent communicating is time not spent accomplishing other tasks so communication must be results-oriented. They may also tend to assume that others are equally busy and only want to know what will help in projects.

The **Individualist** perspective tends toward a growing interest in diversity, relationships, emotional intelligence and internal experience. Because this view is compelled to process more internally, leaders with this perspective are perhaps more likely to select people they believe are open to this type of communication where they can share their internal experience. They will be more focused on context than the earlier developmental perspectives. They tend to seek feedback from various others in a broad range of positions. They are far more likely to share their emotional state with their support team, even sometimes discussing the details of their feelings at length. Because the Individualist view places high importance on communication, leaders in this space are more than likely to articulate events with great detail, often seeking input and buy-in. Other developmental perspectives may perceive this level of communication as excessive.

The **Strategist** perspective is likely to select as advisors a group of peers and stakeholders with different points of view representing the whole system in which they are operating. They may select someone who would appear only moderately successful, but may excel in areas the Strategist leader deeply values as beneficial for team goals. Because their interests have become broader both in terms of global reach and areas of interest, their support teams may also become quite diverse. The Strategist perspective is able to connect with others' specific needs, and thus Strategist communications will often balance a broad range of developmental viewpoints simultaneously. As an outside observer, you will likely see that they communicate more than the Achiever but less than the Individualist. They value both buy-in and accomplishment in a balanced fashion.

Examples and Case Studies

Sample Responses for Jill as a Strategist

The following are Jill's responses to some of the questions. At the Strategist perspective, she is focusing on a broad range of skills, as well as considering her overall development and its impact on her ability to influence the merit of her contributions.

The following section shows the worksheets she completed along with her responses to the reflection questions.

SUPPORT TEAM WORKSHEET – JILL SAMPLE

Goal	Type of Support I Need	Role	Skills/ Knowledge	Arrangement
Increase effectiveness: - Become more adept at seeing multiple perspectives and comfortable with allowing results to emerge rather than controlling	Coach: Alchemist role model	- Gives me exercises and practices. - Provides feedback on behavioral experiments - Open to practicing new behaviors	Multiple-level perspective taking and comfort with ambiguity	Paid Weekly conversations
- Enhance inquiry skills	Spiritual advisor	- Provide ongoing guidance as I apply my daily practice - Enhance my knowledge and understanding of our spiritual traditions	Strong spiritual practice and knowledge of my spiritual traditions	Paid – weekly conversation
Become more emotionally centered and healthier physically	Healthy colleagues	- Reinforce healthy behaviors - Provide feedback on behavioral experiments - Open to practicing new behaviors	Healthy practices	Mutual support
	Healthy friends	- Engage in and reinforce healthy behaviors - Provide feedback on behavioral experiments - Open to practicing new behaviors	Healthy practices	Mutual support

Grow business	Leadership/ business support	▰ Coach/Possible Marketing person ▰ Provide feedback on behavioral experiments	Business growth	Equity in company is possible or paid

The following table is pulled from Jill's Communication Worksheet. You can use it as an example of how one may use communication when managing change both personally and within an organization.

COMMUNICATION PLANNING WORKSHEET – JILL SAMPLE

Who	What to Communicate	What They Can Expect From You	What You Want From Them	How Often
Matthew (spouse)	How am I doing against my major goals? How are my changes impacting you? Us? Practice Inquiry skills	As I become more centered, my reactions to difficult issues will be more thoughtful. As I learn to take more perspectives, I will offer additional insights and also ask questions to better understand his perspective. Additional questions about how my "behavioral experiments" are doing.	Listening Feedback Recommendations	Check in weekly

Leadership Team	How am I doing against my major goals? How are my changes impacting you? Us?	As I become more centered, my reactions to difficult issues will be more thoughtful. As I learn to take more perspectives, I will offer additional insights and also ask questions to better understand their perspectives. Grow the business in ways we jointly define and refine. Additional questions about how my "behavioral experiments" are doing. Discussions that contain additional reflections to provide more context for decision making.	Listening Feedback Recommendations	Check in 2x per month
Friends	I am making some personal changes and I would like feedback as I try new behaviors.	Additional questions about how my "behavioral experiments" are doing. Discussions that contain additional reflections to provide more contexts for decision making.	Feedback Recommendations	Ad Hoc

Jill's Response to Reflection Questions

What do I think/believe?

◼ *What qualities do I want in the people I ask to support my personal change?*

I want a team that understands and values personal growth along with my own development. I find it easier to discuss development when I am talking to someone who resonates with those values. In addition, I want my team to give me candid feedback.

◼ *What qualities will I eliminate from my current and future team?*

This used to be a more theoretical question for me until recently when I stopped associating with one very close friend and member of my development team. This person decided that he needed to manage and advise me rather than support me and trust my judgment even though my choices differed from his. When I asked for a different type of communication, he told me I was wrong and judged me harshly for my request. Because of this experience, I am being much more selective about who I include inside of this process in contrast with those I simply "work with." I realize earlier in my life I allowed people to steer my actions and now I am unwilling to accept this behavior.

As I look at my business partners and their support of my business going forward, I am looking at chemistry, their focus on personal and professional development, their passion for our work and service to our clients and the world. I want to work with people who can move forward through deliberate experiments, who can learn from what we are doing and correct as necessary. They need to be willing to see the best in all of us and address issues from the perspective of a trusted colleague with a willingness to resolve them in a manner that supports mutual success. We will find the balance between personal interest and organizational interest as both needs should be attended to.

◼ *How do I think my change will impact those close to me?*

I hope it will allow me to better serve my clients (both through my catering business and my volunteer work) and work more effectively.

■ *Because my personal development is a very personal and often private choice, what am I willing to communicate to others?*

I believe that my growth and development is a private matter so I only discuss it in depth with people I trust. While I want to model a focus on development, most people do not need to know the details of my goals and plans. Because I am a Partner, it is important to balance what I share and what remains personal. I want to be transparent yet also maintain the level of trust and respect others need.

As I become more comfortable in my current space, I'm more open about sharing my vision with people and finding great support. It is both the vision itself and my passion that I think people are responding to in a very positive manner. I am surprised and delighted to see this reaction. I am not sure why I would think otherwise but that is the case.

■ *Do I need to communicate anything to the organization or just to my support group?*

I am certainly communicating the organizational changes to the organization along with any challenges I face that may ultimately impact them. I want to be sensitive to the commitments of those around me so I focus business meetings on business matters that impact everyone involved. I am not sure where our line will be with regard to personal development and business operations.

However, it is important to me that we are seen as helping the overall community in ways that extend beyond traditional charitable measures (e.g. donating money). As we grow, we are experimenting with ways to promote personal development.

I am shifting how I see myself and the value I bring to the organization. Part of this involves seeing my time as a strategic resource that should be invested in areas that will create value for the business. This means seeing my own value in the world differently. As I see my time as an asset, I can ask where I should invest this time. Given our interest in growing the business, how I invest my time becomes a strategic decision for all involved.

What do I do?

■ *Who do I want to ask to participate in my change?*

I have asked my husband Matthew to be a primary development partner because he knows me better than anyone else. He will also be the most impacted by many of the changes I make.

On the business side, I have asked both a peer on the leadership team and one of the board members I respect. I am looking for different information from each. I have also asked a subordinate that I see as a high potential employee. She will benefit from these discussions since she is focusing on her own development. This will give us an opportunity to work together more closely.

■ *How do I show my conviction through my actions ("walk-the-talk")?*

I believe I walk my talk fairly well. On the business side the biggest and most recent change I have made is to move into the Partner role with this consulting firm. This change requires that I expand my thinking and action to accommodate global concerns. Additionally, I need to consider culture and cross-cultural interactions in ways I did not do in the past. It will be interesting to see how well I perform in this new role and how I can manage learning in this new and often high profile environment. I really want to be successful and minimize public mistakes, yet this new role is a real stretch. I hope to find graceful solutions that will allow me, and all of us, to grow through the process of exploring alternative points of view and different cultures. I realize that is easy to write about and at times quite complicated to do.

■ *How do I convey my request for input and support when I fall short of my stated goals at points along the way?*

This can be quite a delicate situation. It is easy to feel embarrassed when I do not meet my own standards and commitments I have made to others. I have found that with this group, their expectations are not as high as my personal ones, for which I am grateful in some ways and disappointed in others. I am finding profound support for me to take care of myself, and not overextend. This has been so rewarding, simply to work with people who I consider true friends and a wonderful support system. While work continues to have challenges, I love working with people who are able to put differences in perspective aside and see that our challenges are minor relative to our agreements.

What do we believe?

- *Do I have the right support to change the culture of our group to allow me to sustain the changes I am trying to make?*

  Yes, I love the group of people I am working with. Each has amazing qualities and growth opportunities. I trust them and respect them and believe we will collectively support growth of all involved and grow the business. I also acknowledge that any of my colleagues or employees may choose to leave to fulfill their dreams in another place. While I believe this will be difficult for me and for the business, I also want to continue building a culture where people choose to stay because the organization serves them as well as them serving the organization and clients.

- *What are our beliefs about communication with regard to who does the communicating? How much information do they share? How often? Do we solicit input or just convey information?*

  Soliciting input is quite important for me to know what people are doing and what they want refined. Since I joined the consulting firm, I continue to seek a great deal of feedback to understand how much information people want from me, how often, and in what format. For that reason, I try to seek feedback in most of our meetings and conversations. From the input I get, I will create a structured communication plans to help me track what people want and ensure I am meeting their expectations.

How do we do this?

- *What are the key skills and behaviors necessary in my team that support my transformation? What are the gaps between my current support team and the team needed to support transformation? Do I have the right people available with the right skills and behaviors? Do I need to augment my support team with professionals such as a coach, therapist, spiritual advisor, clergy, colleague or boss?*

  On the personal change side, I recently enrolled in a program focused on creating transformative change, an issue of particular importance to me given my interest in world affairs. The program's staff functioned at developmental levels later than mine so that I was able to increase my own perspective taking and see new opportunities for movement.

I augmented my personal development team with a spiritual advisor who helps me find peace and clarity based in my spiritual practices. This has been very important as the developmental process has been very unsettling for me given the enormous shifts in my life in the last 10 years or so. This support has allowed me to find a sense of peace and safety in the world that I lacked and needed to make this transition in an effective and healthy way.

On the business side: I came to see that I needed to augment our team with strategy, global operational skills and cross cultural skills in order to scale and build bridges with diverse stakeholder groups. I have a few people in mind to serve these roles with the right skills.

◼ *What is my communication plan? Who wants feedback? When? Through what medium? From who? What are the key messages? How I keep multiple supporters informed with the right amount of information at the right time to enhance buy-in and influence my behavioral change?*

During my transition, I am defining new communication approaches. I will map communication both internal and external. For now I am communicating with my leadership team, my coach, my spiritual advisor, my husband, and a couple of close friends who I would consider part of my development team. *(See the Table 12)*

Bob's Case study

Bob identified supporters from his professional and family circles to offer various types of feedback and support. As his desired changes were both personal and professional, the communication messages had to work in concert. Communication was not only telling others what he was doing; in addition he sought input and feedback at regular intervals.

His support team included the following:

◼ Professional coach/consultant with a foundation in integral and developmental theory who tested at a developmental level sufficiently later than the client, thereby was able to provide a viewpoint to support his growth. This support included formal coaching and also developing business solutions that were conceived and executed using integral approaches and with the worldview of a Strategist or "Level 5" leader.

- Vistage International, the world's leading chief executive organization, specializing in executive and business coaching for medium and small businesses by providing access to a worldwide network of expert resource speakers, CEO peers, and executive learning workshops. Formerly known as TEC, The Executive Committee, Vistage supports the needs of CEOs by providing a place for chief executives to draw on the experience and knowledge of their peers.

- Wife and Family

- Consultants—other consultants offered point solutions

- Board President of his organization

Bob: I made a point of relating my intentions to improve as a leader and ask for the support of these key individuals. Universally, they were honored to be a confidant and very willing to help. It changed the dynamics of the relationships for the better, as well. My wife thought about what would support my growth along with what she needed from me. My boss not only understood my openness to mean that I respected him and his mentoring, but that I was amenable to change. To him that meant that I would be more manageable and therefore allowed him to relax and trust me more.

His communication focused on the following:

- Personal change goals and actions communicated to the Board, organizational managers, Vistage group, wife and family. For personal development goals, the client not only told people of his goals, he also asked for feedback on his progress. This feedback happened at different intervals and in different formats for the various groups.

- Organizational change goals communicated to the Board, the organizational employees, and consultants. Client established regular communication times, vehicles and norms for each stakeholder group. The messages frequency changed depending on projects in process and the role stakeholders took in each project.

Bob: *I worried that as I began to put my development work into the conversations, that I would be perceived as being too "touchy-feely." Admittedly, not everyone "got" what I was trying to do, although it didn't seem to do any harm to those relationships. Fortunately, I found that those who were further along in their own development were supportive.*

Carl's Case Study

Advisor: During this process, Carl started to consider who he needed on his go-forward team from a personal and professional perspective. We continued to use some key questions to guide his decisions.

On the personal side, Carl and his wife both worked with me as a coach. They are fortunate to have a very strong and supportive relationship so he started his development process with a solid foundation and a wife who supports and encourages him. Additionally, he was meeting others who were looking at things with a similar developmental perspective. During the organizational transition process, he learned that he had other leaders within MT who were operating with more sophisticated views, so he had support inside his company to help him meet his developmental goals.

To address the business acumen goals, Carl was beginning to work with additional consultants to provide specific areas of expertise. One such consultant was a part time CFO to help create more sophisticated financial processes and conduct some analysis needed to launch the new company and move part of the existing company into a new subsidiary. He also continued to communicate with his YPO forum group who helps him meet his business acumen goals. Carl is seeing how his development is helping his YPO Forum group members.

As for the organizational side, this is still a work in process. Carl restructured the organization after he determined he needed to change some of the key participants, alter the roles of others, and modify the way they interacted given the refined organizational direction. He announced the subsidiary company last month and published a new organization chart. While the chart has new titles, the organization is now adjusting to how the work of each executive will change on a daily basis.

Carl chartered a leadership team to make decisions across the enterprise and also put the program management office in place to manage both enterprise level and shared services resources. This will allow everyone to focus on key projects that deliver results against the highest priority goals. This level of structure was new for MT. In the past, they managed the business less formally and while this worked in some ways, the increased need for automation was putting significant stress on the IT organization. This is one part of the business that has expanded during the past year, including hiring a full time person to run the PMO and focusing on process improvement of critical business processes.

Communication is an interesting challenge. Until the leadership team was in agreement, it was not appropriate to communicate much of the efforts going on. This created some concerns as people were seeing changes. Carl began sending a monthly newsletter, having one-on-one meetings with his direct reports weekly, and going to the various locations to meet with their leadership teams monthly. He is spending a much greater part of his time communicating and people still want to know more. We are continuing to look for additional ways to keep people informed and involved while balancing their need to focus on their work.

Your Individual Process to Build Your Team and Communicate

Now that you have read through these personal narratives, it is time to complete the worksheets and answer the questions in Table 9-3 for yourself. We encourage you to complete all of the exercises. This chapter serves to help you clarify your supporters and communication plan while you begin defining your feedback sources. This is the plan that will provide you support for your development, in terms of expertise, emotional support, buy-in, and feedback.

This chapter summarizes the basics for creating a support and communication plan. While this may seem extraneous, never underestimate the value of both emotional and moral support and communication to those impacted by your changes. This could be as simple as talking to your spouse or family about the way your changing routine may impact them, while letting them know you appreciate their willingness to be flexible.

CHAPTER 10:

Take Action

Figure 10-1 Innovative Leadership Development Process

Now that you have created a plan to become an innovative leader, it is time to implement your plan of action. As you begin realizing your vision, you will also identify challenges to your growth and development. Barriers are simply a normal part of any transformative process, and we have provided a number of useful tools to help pinpoint and navigate them successfully using each of the quadrants.

An important part of your success during this stage is believing that you can make and sustain growth in your leadership capacity and capability. You developed a strong foundation by creating a compelling vision and analyzed unique challenges and opportunities to determine what actions you needed to take to achieve your goals. It is now time to further implement your plan with the support of your team. Be aware that this stage can take tremendous focus and energy. Many people lose their focus here, especially when the change process becomes difficult and the demands of balancing life requirements take greater urgency. Think, for example, of how many times you may have joined a gym and yet did not follow your plan to go there a certain number of times per week. Implementing a plan requires a deep commitment to your growth and also an understanding of the barriers you will face based on your personality type or history with implementing change. As barriers surface, you have the ability to remove them or modify your course with the support of your team.

With this in mind, allow yourself some flexibility in the growth process instead of viewing your plan as fixed. See your plan as an initial starting point, or a working hypothesis about how you will develop. Along these lines, you can better use the challenges you will face as a way to provide feedback on your original hypothesis and modify it as you go along. In other words, rather than viewing these obstacles as threats, you have the opportunity to naturally incorporate them as fine-tuning mechanisms. For each challenge you face, carefully consider the unique learning opportunity and how to use it to help you implement your plan. Since personal development is a long-term journey, you will have many opportunities to face these challenges and take corrective actions.

Lastly, your support team will play a crucial role in helping to make the plan sustainable. They will offer you input and feedback as well as encouragement during times when you may struggle. Even though you specifically chose the changes and goals within your plan, it is often still helpful to have a built in system of accountability. When you run into inner resistance and difficulty, connect with someone who will remind you that you are already competent and that you can meet these goals in the same way you have met many other challenges.

Tools

The following worksheet helps you to anticipate barriers and mitigate them while implementing your action plan. You can refer to Jill's completed worksheets for an example.

TABLE 10-1: BARRIERS ACTION PLANNING WORKSHEET

Category	Barrier	Impact of barrier	How to remove or work around it	Support I need to remove or work around
In my thinking				
In my behavior				
In our beliefs				
In how we do things				

Innovative Leadership Reflection Questions

To help you develop your action plan, it is time to further clarify your direction using reflection questions. These questions are organized by quadrant to reflect the four native domains introduced in Section I. As a reminder, this is an opportunity to practice innovative leadership by considering how your change plan will affect changes in your intentions, actions, culture and systems. The questions are arranged to help you explore each of these domains. The "What do I think/believe?" questions reflect your intentions. The "What do I do?" questions reflect your actions. The "What do we believe?" questions reflect culture. The "How do we do this?" questions reflect systems. This exercise is designed to help you practice innovative leadership as you create your vision and define your direction.

TABLE 10-2: QUESTIONS TO GUIDE THE LEADER AND ORGANIZATION

What do I think/ believe?

- In what ways do I need to change my perspective or skills to succeed?
- What new skills do I need to gain beyond those planned?
- What do I need to change about how I see myself or the world to become more effective?
- Including beliefs, what do I need to let go of to make these changes?
- What do I see as my individual role? How does this role allow me to fit in different organizations including my family?
- How can I grow effectively and empower myself? How do I support my success as well as the success of the organization(s)?
- How can I benefit from my own personal growth and development?

What do I do?

- What feedback do I seek that will allow me to correct, redirect or recalibrate my behavior and feel motivated to make the necessary changes?

- How do I request clear and concise feedback that allows me to grow and supports the growth of others?

- How do I determine what I am ready to change within myself and what additional support I require for those changes I am resisting?

- What help am I willing to request? Am I investing appropriate time and/or money to support my growth? Is the commitment I am making to my personal change consistent with the results I am expecting to receive?

- What creative solutions can I find to increase my personal awareness? Do I track my performance against my goals using logs or refection activities?

- How will I identify times when my own behavior undermines my success?

- What will I do when I find my own behavior undermines my success?

- Can I treat my own competing commitments as learning opportunities?

- How do I encourage bad news as well as good from my support team?

- Am I looking for opportunities to visibly demonstrate my progress as my development process unfolds?

- What am I doing to retain my support team as time goes on?

- How do I manage my transformation as time goes on? How do I focus on living my current life while concurrently focusing sufficient time on my vision and goals?

What do we believe?

- How will my changes impact my ability to be successful based on the organization's reward system given its values, goals, and culture?

- What are the stories within the organization about effective leadership? How do my personal changes position me going forward?

- What stories of the past do we need to stop telling because they no longer support our or my success?

- How can we connect prior leadership development successes to my current development effort? How can we use prior success to reinforce our ability to navigate current leadership changes?

- What part of our past failures was attributed to leadership? Do my development changes appear positive to the organization's success or are they threatening?

- Does our culture support the behavioral traits I am trying to develop?

How do we do this?

- What processes do we have that may serve as barriers to my developing in the way I would like? Am I in a position to change the systems to remove these barriers? If so, how involved and complex will those changes be? If I cannot remove the barriers, how will I navigate around them?

- Are my changes aligned with the organization's guiding principles? If not, how do I navigate the gaps between them?

- Do the organizational structure and governance approach support my personal development? If not, what options do I have to resolve barriers to my growth?

- What early warning metrics can I track to let me know what impact my behavioral changes are having on others? What leading indicators will alert me before any significant issues arise?

- How can I leverage current or generally accepted mastery frameworks to gain support of others and explain the changes I am trying to make?

- How do my changes fit into the current organizational reward system? If there are misalignments, what will I do to navigate the barriers and challenges?

- Have I clearly articulated the changes I want to make and asked for the support of those around me while allowing them to maintain their success in a dynamic and changing environment?

- What communication processes do we use to provide timely feedback? How will these impact me during my development? How will my development impact others?

- What communication, if any, do I use for those who are not supporting my development?

- What is the organization doing to measure, communicate, and fund my development and activities?

Analysis of Developmental Perspectives

The leader at the **Expert** perspective wants to do things right. He or she is likely to follow a well-structured plan and stick to it. At this leadership perspective, one may begin to struggle when not seeing expected results or not meeting personal standards following the plan. Since the Expert is focused on doing tasks properly, he or she will be frustrated if unable to perform tasks as planned.

The leader at the **Achiever** perspective sees the need to move more decisively forward with less attention to the change's impact on others and less focus on the impact of the organization. The barriers they are likely to face involve over-commitment and burn out.

The leader at the **Individualist** perspective sees the need to spend more time gaining input and acceptance from others about the impacts of these changes. Additionally, since those at the Individualist perspective appear more compelled toward loosely following rules or structure, they will probably not adhere to their plan very well. If the plan is solid and the leader deviates significantly, he or she may not realize the expected results. Individualists may use this opportunity to get to know themselves better, naturally allowing the process of introspection to flow beyond planning. Leaders at this perspective may benefit from being open to revising the plan based on self-reflection.

The leader at the **Strategist** perspective sees the need to gather input balanced with a strong inclination toward setting the course and being responsible for accomplishing the results that pull them. The Strategist will balance the focus on process and projected results by aligning with overall vision.

Sample Responses for Jill as a Strategist

Once again, we've created responses to the worksheet and some of the questions from Jill's perspective as a Strategist. It is important to answer 1-3 questions from each quadrant in the attached tables of reflection questions.

BARRIER ACTION PLANNING WORKSHEET – JILL SAMPLE				
Category	Barrier	Impact of barrier	How to remove or work around it	Support I need to remove or work around
In my thinking	I think I will never really meet my goals	I give up too soon	Go to a friend to remind me I can and also report in so I feel external pressure when I want to give up	Continue to talk to friend weekly to reinforce that I can meet these goals
In my behavior				
In our beliefs				
In how we do things	We reward behavior that just gets things done	Expectations of action based on speed without full analysis	Remember that my full presence is required for us to be effective	Find others on the team with similar developmental level and working style and reinforce one another

Jill's response to Reflection Questions

What do I think/believe?

- *In what ways do I need to change my perspective or skills to succeed?*

One of my development goals is to expand my ability to see additional perspectives. To grow, I will need to continue to participate in exercises that require me to take multiple perspectives such as the shadow exercise where I look at situations from the perspective of others involved. Perspective taking is a skill I am working to develop as part of my goals. I will know if I have done this well when I track my progress based on input of others. While this is important work, it is also hard to continue to seek out my own shortcomings. I will do this at a pace I can manage.

Accomplishing this goal may help me build the foundation to becoming more effective. Coincidentally, it may also help me move to a later developmental level. From a skills perspective, I believe I need to continue my personal growth and expand my own ways of dealing with other individuals at various developmental levels.

What do I do?

- *How do I determine what I am ready to change within myself and what additional support I require for those changes I am resisting?*

One of the exercises I have found most effective to answer this question is the "competing commitment" exercise in the book: *How the Way We Talk Can Change the Way We Work: Seven Languages for Transformation* by Robert Kegan and Lisa Laskow Lahey (Dec 16, 2002) where I identify what I say I am committed to and what I am unconsciously committed to that may undermine what I say.

One issue I have that competes with my commitment of personal and business growth is the image I have of myself as being not smart enough to lead an organization so I need to work harder than anyone else to make sure no one finds out about my deficiencies. This belief has led me to be a workaholic and be a bit unbalanced. As long as I continue to hold a view of myself as less than competent, I will continue to act in manners that undermine my success such as hoping that I really do not need to speak in front of many people, etc. To address these fears, I am taking small steps to test my assumptions about my limitations. I am now speaking to different stakeholder groups and seeking input from my mentors about my offerings and leadership capabilities. The list of experiments goes on.

In each small experiment, I disprove my assumption that I am not smart enough or that I am being arrogant to try. In addition to disproving my fears, I actively reflect on what I intend (grow the organization, expand general knowledge, etc.), my strategies (the actions I take such as publishing articles), practices (meditation), and results (business getting additional recognition). Through an ongoing inquiry of my effectiveness, I am learning to remove my own barriers from my thinking. These action and reflection cycles range from major intentions such as the direction of my business down to my intention for a 1 hour meeting or a conversation. These action and reflection cycles allow me to see more clearly what is working and also what assumptions and beliefs I hold that are incomplete or inaccurate.

- *What clear, concise feedback do I seek that will allow me to correct, redirect or recalibrate my behavior and feel motivated to make the necessary changes?*

I seek several types of feedback ranging from asking my employees how they are responding to my experiment to asking valued stakeholders to let me know what is working and what is not. They are able to tell me if they think I understand their perspective and what I could do to provide them better service. I believe I often seek feedback as a source of information that allows me to accurately reflect on my progress.

Additionally, since some of my goals are best discussed with a friend rather than a professional colleague, I selected a close friend to give me feedback about our interactions. She is also engaged in her own journey of development so we share stories about what is working and what we are struggling with. When I am having a bad day, I trust her to tell me if the challenges I am facing are likely something I need to work harder on. We talk about our goals and track our progress with one another so I feel somewhat motivated to do what I say so I do not need to tell her I missed the goal. This accountability really helps me stay focused. She is also a great support in that she believes deeply in my ability. She continues to remind me how I have overcome obstacles in the past and how I will continue to do so in the future. Her friendship and support really makes this adventure much easier.

What do we believe?

■ *How will my changes impact my ability to be successful based on the organizations reward system given its values, goals, and culture?*

I am fortunate to be a Partner of the organization so my changes should not impact my ability to keep my job. They will however impact those with whom I work and possibly impact the overall organizational culture. The changes I am experiencing now and expect to continue to experience are changing our goals and overall business offerings and our culture is changing. Our culture is being refined as we clarify our goals and service offerings in the context of an ever changing economic conditions and emerging political changes.

■ *What are the stories within the organization about effective leadership?*

One of our stories about effective leadership is that as leaders we must be very flexible and be able to both set long term goals and also plan our short term activities based on what we see emerging in our environment. This balance of both long term general direction and short term dynamic steering is viewed as a critical skill in effective leaders.

How do we do this?

■ *Do the organizational structure and the governance approach support my personal development? If not, what options do I have to remove barriers to my growth?*

One of the governance approaches we take is the idea of dynamic steering. We have a business plan and overall direction. From there, we tend to make small decisions and corrective actions that we treat as experiments. Dynamic steering is a foundation from a larger system called Holacracy and is similar to the process of steering a bicycle, we know where we are going and the ride is much smoother if we make small corrections in direction on an ongoing basis rather than sharp corrections. This sounds pretty basic but I have found it is a real shift in the way most organizations operate. It means we need to be willing to question and change our decisions regularly. It also means the corrections that happen are small ones.

We tend to treat most decisions as learning opportunities. This means we try to develop a hypothesis or idea of what will work and test it. In each test we learn and refine our thinking. By taking this approach – an action and reflection cycle for the business, we are able to continually learn. This process is quite aligned with my personal approach to my development and also allows me freedom to try my own new behaviors in the business as experiments. I can experiment with different roles or approaches and learn from these experiments.

The others in the organization have the same opportunity and freedom to try new approaches and offer recommendations. We generally have a bias to try anything unless we believe an experiment could have an adverse impact on the organization.

Bob's Case Study

Bob actively pursued his short term and long term plans. He met with his coach/consultant weekly to track progress and refine the plan. These regular meetings provided both structure and discipline to the process. The content of the meetings changed as organizational and individual needs changed. In each meeting, time was allocated for discussion of the client's personal development. Depending on the other priorities, these discussions were minimal. Once the key transition activities were complete, the client again focused primarily on his development.

Bob: There is a real value to having weekly reality checks. I knew that a meeting with the coach was coming up and I would have to be honest about what I was doing. More than the value of this action "deadline," was the value of stopping what I was doing once a week and being brutally honest with myself. What was I doing? Was I really doing what I intended? How was that working for me? What needed to change? If I had I been meeting only once a month with the coach, I am sure a lot of things would have gotten off track.

The personal development actions included:

- *Mentoring/coaching by individual with developmental level Strategist or later*

- *Competing Commitments exercise and follow-on observations*

- *Practice Action Inquiry techniques as defined by Bill Torbert & Associates in their book Action Inquiry*

- *Practice Noticing exercises: pay attention to assumptions, feelings and behaviors that would otherwise pass you by. This will generally be after the fact.*

- *Pay attention to how unique individual circumstances and needs impact your ability to accomplish goals. How do these factors impact other's abilities to accomplish goals?*

- *Review and refine career goals and direction*

- *Read books and publications that support development: Action Inquiry by Torbert and Associates, How the Way We Talk can Change Way We Work by Kegan and Lahey, and Review developmental levels information provided by Cook-Greuter as part of the MAP Assessment feedback package*

- *Re-engage in meditation and deep spiritual practice*

- *Re-engage with friends*

- *Take up an enjoyable activity: golf*

- *Continue to volunteer on a Board of Directors for a land preservation not-for-profit organization*

- *Journal*

- *Weight lifting*

The organizational change actions included:

- *Developing an agreed upon set of annual objectives and a way to evaluate success. This activity allowed the leader to expand his view of the organization, understand the perspective of the board, create a structure that provided continuity across years and establish board rotations.*

- *Creating guiding principles to serve as the basis for an employee manual and needed cultural change. This activity allowed the leader to create a culture that aligned and supported the organization's long term goals.*

- *Defining and implementing changes to business processes necessary to support a growing dynamic international organization. The leader evaluated organizational risk and created systems and processes that supported the goals established by the organization.*

- *Creating a plan for both internal and external communications. The leader expanded his view of critical stakeholders and took a proactive approach in determining what information would support both stakeholder and the organizational success.*

- *Creating an interview process and guidelines for behavioral interviewing to ensure candidates were selected for both skills and cultural fit with the organization. The client proactively determined that he needed to ensure future employees not only demonstrated the skills necessary to perform the tasks, they also needed to demonstrate behaviors consistent with the organization's culture and values.*

- *Assisting in assessing the business risks and developing solutions to mitigate them. This risk assessment was one of the foundation tools to guide all other projects to ensure client service remained high and risks were mitigated during growth and transitions.*

Carl's Case Study

Advisor: While we have a step called "Take Action," Carl was taking action during the entire process. At some point, his primary focus eventually shifted from planning to implementation, which was a fairly recent change. On the personal side he had been practicing Action Inquiry concepts for several months while he was putting a plan in place for the organization.

Going into the process, our approach was to focus our energies where people were willing to change and take advantage of situations as they arose to serve as platforms for change. While this may have appeared less structured than a traditional change, it allowed Carl to address much of the individual and organizational resistance that was emerging. Like tai chi, it allowed him to use the energy of the leaders of MT to set the course. When barriers arose, we acknowledged them and made conscious decisions on how to deal with them.

Initially, there was no strong pull to create a vision. Instead, Carl focused on creating processes in key areas such as accounting and implementing the PMO. When the new company was launched, it became clearer that the leaders of the organization needed to work together differently than they had before. Another catalyst was the promotion of a short-tenure leader to run the new company. This event focused the existing General Managers on the need for leadership development in addition to exceptional business performance.

The following is a worksheet that represents the type of analysis we considered when deciding how to proceed during key challenges. The biggest challenge I saw was getting the leaders of the core business to support the new direction. They did share Carl's sense of urgency or vision for the future. The decision to launch a new company was primarily a result of Carl's response to some significant barriers faced while trying to both run the core business and launch a new set of services.

This is one place where the family business issues arose. The President of MT had been working for the company since Carl was 6 years old. He is a very competent and committed man and his skills are a significant reason MT became such a successful company. Now, Carl had purchased the company and had a very different approach. One challenge I observed was that because Carl grew up with MT, many of the senior leaders saw him as he developed over his life. They remembered some of his youthful mistakes and I believe that impacted his credibility. In addition, after he purchased the company, he agreed that to make the transition easier, his dad would continue to run the company for 2 years. Thus, when Carl began to take control, many people had been going to his father as the owner for 30 years and lacked a clear definition of who was actually in power. Carl needed to establish himself as the leader and manage a respectful transition while his dad continued to work at the company. This transition is still taking place. There appears to be a delicate balance required to honor the people who built the company while making changes to how the company is run.

Carl: As I mentioned earlier, one of my greatest challenges was an organization that had not acceptance that I was now in charge. Since my father still works at the company, people would naturally gravitate towards him about any and all issues regarding the company or worse, "concerns" about the direction I was taking the company. This is a no-win proposition, as it made it impossible for me to stay on top of things if managers were going to him instead of engaging me. Further, in their minds, dad was still "running the company" which was not creating sustainability if I was supposed to be learning the ropes and guiding the company in a new direction. What it would do is leave us in management "no man's land" as people would oscillate between whichever style they liked that day. After he realized how this was disruptive to the company and undermined my ability to lead the organization, he began sending people directly to me rather than tackle the issues himself.

I also received tremendous pressure from my senior leadership team about rocking the boat. These guys had been part of the company since I was in first grade. They are the ones who made the company successful, and helped to feed, clothe and educate our family while we were growing up. They help to pay my salary today. They had sold and serviced everything from the liquid toner copiers of the early 1970's to the high tech networks and connected devices we handle today. They had helped us grow from one location to seven locations. They moved themselves and their families from city to city because we needed them to do so. They had literally increased the annual revenue 100 times in 35 years. Their loyalty to the company is of heroic proportion. Who was I to question them? Not that they were arrogant, just highly experienced in our industry. So, who was I supposed to believe? One of the most difficult obstacles was deciding between "theory" and "proven history." My gut told me the theory made good sense, and I believed it to be a well thought out plan. It promised to deliver results. "Salvation is in the future," the plan beckoned. Essentially, I had to choose between the experience of Senior Leadership, which said "Don't change because you have a good thing going here" and the theory which suggested "If you don't apply this theory and change, your company will be gone in five years." On one hand, I wanted to respect the history, but on the other hand I knew these were different times.

For the first time in 15 years, we were not experiencing double-digit growth. Credit was getting tight, so it was getting harder to finance our customers. I was told more than once per day, "This leadership stuff is time consuming, expensive and disruptive, especially in economic times like these. If you want to increase profits around here, try focusing on increased sales and cut our costs by getting rid of those expensive consultants." Short term, that's mathematically correct, however they could not account for why margins and profits were slipping long before the consultants arrived. Worse, there was no plan to right the ship - just keep doing what has worked in the past and work harder until this economic situation blows over. Hope is not a strategy I like to employ. What kept me in the "Theory" game was the realization that things were heading south and none of the senior managers had a viable plan. The exercises my advisor and I undertook continually revealed holes in the current "plan" or lack thereof. It showed the weaknesses in our processes. It showed that we were not making decisions based on the data, but rather our flawed intuition. Our leadership team was not accustomed to using the data to make strategic decisions. When things were good, we smiled and thought we must be doing it right, but when things were slipping, we just assured ourselves that next month would be better. Yes, I lost sleep wondering if I was just an ideological punk, intoxicated by the false promises of Theory Redemption or if I was actually creating long term sustainability and my efforts would be realized in the future.

Your Process of Taking Action

Now that you have read Jill's narrative responses and commentary from Bob, and Carl, it is time to complete the worksheets and answer the questions in the Table 10-2 for yourself. We encourage you to complete all of the exercises and answer 1-3 questions from each quadrant in the reflection question exercise.

CHAPTER 11:
Embed Innovation Systematically

Figure 11-1 – Innovative Leadership Development Process

Congratulations! You have made it to the final step in your development process; you are now ready to shift from implementing your plan as something with a discreet end to considering how you will integrate these changes into your lifestyle going forward. We suggest your view your leadership development as an ongoing process rather than something to check off the to-do list. Given the volume of change we are facing now and expect to face in the future, continual development is a must – just to keep current. In this light, you can begin asking yourself: "What supports can I put into place to stay on track? How can I gain additional benefits from ongoing practice?

To maintain momentum, it is critical to retain a sense of urgency while minimizing the sense of comfort that may come from early success. Be aware that it is easy to stray from your goals if you declare success based on your early results, especially when other areas of your life tug at your time and attention. One helpful shift in thinking is to see the actions you are taking as a practice. You are practicing your leadership skills in the same fashion that a professional athlete practices a particular sport. The most successful athletes are constantly practicing to improve, even though they may already be the best in the world. This is also why many of them remain successful as leaders. You will need to consider making time in the long term for activities that best foster success and help maintain your support system.

Therefore, ask yourself: "When I see progress, what will keep me going in my ongoing practice? I need some reminder that my progress is a result of engaged practice, and my performance is likely to suffer if I do not maintain a proper focus."

Additionally, by this point, you may want to re-evaluate your goals and begin raising the bar. You will need to balance establishing a long-term practice to sustain progress while identifying your next developmental focus or goals.

Altogether, this chapter invites you to of be more conscious of actions as well as tangible barriers. Identify the elements in your life that support the continual realization of your goals; also, examine the events and relationships that interfere with your vision and goals. It is critical to remove as many barriers as possible and to stop behaviors that no longer align with your development goals.

Thus, the overall purpose here is to understand your habits and choices and ensure they are aligned with your long-term goals.

Tools

Below is a table you can use to capture and track your progress. For many people, the simple action of recording their progress in writing helps maintain their commitments. Use the following worksheet to help you track your progress against each of your goals. If you would like to see a sample, please review Jill's answers later in this chapter.

TABLE 11-1 PERSONAL TRANSFORMATION ACTIVITY/ PRACTICE LOG TEMPLATE

Goal	Action	Record Actual Performance	Expected Impact	Priority	Measure	Progress	Feedback From Who
Top 1	1.						
	2.						
	3.						
Top 2	4.						
	5.						
	6.						
Top 3	7.						
	8.						
	9.						

Innovative Leadership Reflection Questions

To help you develop your action plan, it is time to further clarify your direction, using reflection questions. These questions are organized by quadrant to reflect the four native domains introduced in Section I. As a reminder, this is an opportunity to practice innovative leadership by considering how your change plan will affect changes in your intentions, actions, culture, and systems. These questions are arranged to help you explore each of these domains. The questions for "What do I think/believe?" reflect your intentions. The questions "What do I do?" reflect your actions. The questions "What do we believe?" reflect culture. The questions "How do we do this?" reflect systems. Thus, we designed this exercise to help you start practicing innovative leadership as you create your vision and define your direction.

TABLE 11-2: QUESTIONS TO GUIDE THE LEADER AND ORGANIZATION

What do I think/ believe?

- How do I honor the progress I have made while maintaining focus on the balance of the work that needs to be done?
- How do I deal with both profound progress and a need for continued change?
- How do I deal with unresolved issues and uncertainty as I move forward?
- How do I deal with my desire to fix this issue and get back to the real work
- What progress have I made as a leader/person?
- Are my assumptions still valid?
- As I have changed, am I still in the right role for my personal values and mission?
- How do I define myself as a leader? How do I think about my role and impact? How does my story about my effectiveness support or hinder my continued success?
- How does my belief about myself differ from how others see me?
- Am I still committed to the practices I developed?
- Am I willing to make these practices part of my life-long term?

What do I do?

- What do I communicate that conveys both progress and continued urgency?

- Am I visibly doing what I have committed to doing?

- Am I living up to the standards I have set for myself?

- Am I perceived as acting with integrity, with regard to meeting my commitments?

- What do I do that reinforces the impact of my personal development?

- What do I do to sustain my new practices and development?

- How am I continuing to show the new behaviors I have publically and privately committed to?

- How do I continue to sustain the practices I have started and behavioral changes I have made? Have these changes become part of who I am, or will I slowly slide back to old behaviors – especially under stress or as other priorities emerge?

- Do I surround myself with others who are focused on their personal changes so that I have a reinforcement system?

- Do I continue to track and measure my progress?

What do we believe?

- What do we believe about people who are always focused on their development?

- What do we believe about ongoing development practices vs. fixing problems then moving on?

- What do we believe about how to monitor and build momentum in different areas of life?

- What do we believe about appropriate pace and focus on development and growth?

- How do our beliefs about growth impact our ability to maintain momentum?

- What recognition is appropriate from different groups in my life (family, work)?

- How do we see ourselves now? How has our image of ourselves changed based on my personal change?

- Will the organization's goals and values change based on my personal changes?

- How do we react to old behaviors that no longer support the organization?

- If our organizational stories about who we are change, do we incorporate new jargon, best practices, and human interest into emerging organizational stories?

How do we do this?

- What are the top 3 new behaviors others can expect to see? How will these behaviors be measured and reinforced?

- Who will remind me I can make the changes when I am struggling?

- Do I clearly understand how my personal changes impact my work? Have I started to change the way I do my job? Have I informed others (discussed with others) how their jobs or tasks will change based on my changes? If my changes impact how we interact, have we agreed on the new way we will work together? Are we following a structured plan to consistently perform according to new structure or guidelines?

- Do we need training to support new behaviors or interactions?

- What happens if I am not successful in meeting my top three goals? How would I like others to reinforce and/or support my behavioral changes?

- Do we have systems in place that discourage me successfully accomplishing my top three goals?

- What processes/measures will we establish to identify behaviors that are no longer appropriate or necessary? What can I stop doing that will give me more time to practice?

- Are there any additional ways to gain additional momentum to leverage existing changes and/or small wins?

- Am I reviewing measures regularly and recognizing results toward my change goals?

- Does the organization acknowledge leaders who have made the desired changes (job starts and stops) and mastered new skills? Am I being rewarded for my personal development in this system?

- Do we continue to measure and reward actions that are necessary to sustain the changes using the updated job descriptions and process metrics? Am I still a good fit within this system?

- Has the organization rewarded me with recognition, promotion, increased responsibilities, or financial rewards?

- Will others be expected to demonstrate behaviors and skills that I developed during my change? How will their changed behavior reinforce my new skills and behaviors?

- Have we sufficiently updated employee orientations and other human resources and IT systems to support changes in goals and values for our leaders?

- Are we reviewing objective and subjective measures regularly and recognizing desired leadership behaviors for myself and others?

- Are we reinforcing actions that positively influence the larger vision while inquiring into those that do not?

- Have we developed and tracked success?

Analysis of Developmental Perspectives

The **Expert** perspective focuses on gathering facts and data. When leaders take this perspective, they become interested in perfecting the skills associated with their craft. They continue to develop their technical skills. They are quite concerned with measuring their success and demonstrating to others what they have accomplished. They want to be known as the expert in their fields. The education they seek tends to be rule oriented rather than focused on building inner capacity for personal judgment or independent thought.

The **Achiever** perspective focuses on development as long as this focus is supported by observable success against valued measures. Effective measures and rewards help the Achiever stay focused and reinforce the growth they have already realized. There is always the possible distraction of diverting focus to the next priority and subsequently loosing focus on development. The Achiever perspective is likely to see growth as another static goal to accomplish, with the intention of simply moving upon completion instead of viewing development as a long-term practice.

The **Individualist** lens also has access to a wide range of skills, concerning the capacity for introspection and self-reflection. While taking this perspective, leaders are likely to engage in action-reflection cycles (taking action, checking the results, then starting over again) that allow them to increase effectiveness in outcomes, practices, and strategies. They may really enjoy focusing on their development, and they may seek others who have a similar focus. However, this leader perspective may also fail to gain sufficient momentum if overly concerned with building a support team to create change, all the while marginalizing the real action required for transformation. Because the Individualist view is prone to pushing horizons and rules, this thinking may resist the idea of a structured long-term practice. This may often feel very confining, so a leader with this perspective will likely seek something that is more flexible.

Finally, the **Strategist** perspective is likely able to see the mission, processes, and tasks that need to unfold in a relatively seamless and complimentary fashion. The potential of the Strategist view is competent at seeing overall goals and finding an effective approach to meet those goals. A leader operating from this point of view has access to a wide range of skills and thought processes that correspondingly support personal development. The Strategist view has an immense ability to navigate through multiple complex situations that in turn create reflective feedback, which supports growth opportunities. The growing edge for the Strategist may be letting go of the need to perform or control performance, in favor of allowing space for development to take its own shape in alignment with the larger world. A Strategist leader will benefit from trusting more and controlling less, knowing that there is some innate intelligence built into every process, and that by simply standing back and allowing themselves and others to travel their paths, amazing and unforeseen things will unfold.

Examples and Case Studies

Sample Responses for Jill as a Strategist

Once again, we've created responses to some of the questions from Jill's perspective as a Strategist. Here is an example of a Personal Transformation Activity Log for Jill and her goals.

TABLE 11-1 PERSONAL TRANSFORMATION ACTIVITY/ PRACTICE LOG TEMPLATE

Goal	Action	Record Actual Performance	Expected Impact	Priority	Measure	Progress	Feedback From Who
Top 1	1. Meditate 10 min/ day	Mon - 10 min Tues - none Wed - none Thurs - 5 min Friday - 20 min	Calming Composure, Emotional Balance	1	Frequency of meeting goal	Met goal 3x this week	Spouse – impact of calm Colleague - impact of composure
	2. Action Inquiry Daily						
	3.						

Jill's reflection Question Responses

What do I think/believe?

- *How do I honor the progress I have made while maintaining focus on the balance of the work that needs to be done?*

  In some areas, my progress encourages me to go forward, while in others, the changes I am making scare me, thus causing me to experience a sense of regression. Still, I am making progress in my ability to take additional perspectives and being more adept at looking at my competing commitments. In some ways, I am really excited about these new insights I am finding and also excited about letting go of old fears and old behaviors. I feel so relieved. As I say this, I also realize much of my behavior is based on old habits. I need to be very attentive to making decisions out of habit or fear.

  I am trying to be both aware and gentle with myself. If I am experiencing an adjustment time associated with a new perspective or skill, I have come to learn that I can expect to revert back to old coping mechanisms until I master the new ability. These mechanisms are like old friends, and I have come to find safety and comfort in them, knowing that they will pass over time and I can continue to focus on my growth.

  I believe that I will continue to focus on my own growth over the balance of my life. The level of focus will ebb and flow based on other life events and circumstances. I do trust that I will continue this path because I hold my own growth as a core belief about who I am and how I live my life.

- *What progress have I made as a leader/person? Are my assumptions still valid?*

  I believe I have made significant progress toward becoming more conscious of my behaviors and practices and how they impact my intentions. I have also made great progress in balancing my life. As I have made these changes, I am seeing that my assumptions are still valid and that my direction is still appropriate for me. With the dynamic steering approach, I believe I have the freedom to change my daily course of action while maintaining my overall direction.

I am committed to turning the actions in my plan into ongoing life practices. I can see that I am much more effective as a person and as a leader when I make time to care for myself, including sleep, diet, exercise, and meditation. I am also more compassionate and easier to work with when I take the time to consider problems and opportunities from many different perspectives, including the perspective of the person I may think is causing me this problem.

What do I do?

- *What do I communicate that conveys both progress and continued urgency?*

Probably the best way for me to communicate my urgency is through my actions. I actively participate in a personal-development practice. I communicate this practice and ask for feedback. My main sources of feedback professionally are my employees. We work very closely together, so they are able to provide a daily perspective.

Additionally, I continue to work with a coach who is significantly more advanced developmentally. He is able to offer insights, recommend practices, and help me maintain my focus. In some ways, I feel accountable to him since he has agreed to be my coach.

- *What do I do to sustain my new practices and development? How am I continuing to show the new behaviors I have publically and privately committed to?*

I have found my personal reflection practice has turned into a regular habit. My colleagues are also using this practice, so it has become part of what we do. My meditation practice has always been important, I continue to value this time, and I find it even more important than I imagined in the past, in order to allow me to stay centered and feel competent as the business grows and changes. On days when I am tired and do not feel like meditating, I remember that it is this practice that allows me to navigate life's difficult challenges with some level of grace and ease. The connection I make between the activity of meditation and the value it provides me on a daily basis keeps me committed even when I would rather not because of time or other life pressures.

Our business team looks to me to be confident that we can meet our goals and that we will all be called to experiment with new approaches and behaviors to meet the ever-changing needs of the market and the world.

What do we believe?

- *What do we believe about appropriate pace and focus on development and growth?*

The people in my new organization place a significant emphasis on personal growth. This is one of the values we hold very high in our overall culture. This means we ask for and provide feedback, and also make time to discuss development goals and strategies to support one another. While the company does not overtly require participation in personal development initiatives, being around others who are heavily focused on developing creates a subtle pressure to maintain individual advancements.

- *How do we see ourselves now? How has our image of ourselves changed based on my personal change?*

As an organization, we see ourselves as leaders in the area of global organizational effectiveness and sustainability initiatives. Our image as a collective organization is improving because I have developed a clearer image of who I am and what I can contribute to it. Additionally, the organization has a clearer view of who it is and what it does in the world.

We are also highly committed to individual and group development. We have revisited our guiding principles, and we have confirmed that this value is part of what has enabled us to be successful while also creating an environment we enjoy working in. We see this focus as a differentiator, and it is very important for all of us.

How do we do this?

- *What are the top 3 new behaviors others can expect to see? How will these behaviors be measured and reinforced?*

- Become more **conscious** of my behaviors and their impact on others, along with their alignment with my stated intention. Measure based on feedback from others and the absence of drama in my personal and professional life. Also note the absence of discussions where I am surprised about how I impacted others (positively or negatively).

- Feeling **calm and centered** in a way that will allow me to relate to others without distraction from either wandering thoughts or emotions, thereby influencing my ability to focus on the topic at hand. Measure based on my personal evaluation of how effectively I am performing and how often I feel distracted and unable to stay focused on the task at hand.

- Ongoing **small experiments** focused on growing the business. Measure business growth by brand awareness, number of clients, client volume, and client satisfaction.

- *Does the organization acknowledge leaders who have made the desired changes (job starts and stops) and mastered new skills? Am I being rewarded for my personal development in this system?*

The organization does acknowledge leaders who make the desired changes. If leaders are not making the necessary changes, the organization tries to find a place where the leader can fit and add value. The value they add must be appropriate to their compensation and the energy invested by other team members supporting their change and supporting their participation on the team.

I am being rewarded because the organization is thriving and I am gaining roles with increasing opportunity to impact the world in ways I find important. I have a role within the organization that allows me to do the work I love to do and make sufficient money to feel comfortable with my lifestyle.

We have also started to interview and select employees based on their fit into our culture. Since we all value physical and emotional health, as well as interacting with one another in a manner that respects differing points of view, we have created a rigorous interview process that selects candidates with these qualities and weeds out people who would not be supportive of these values. We believe that we will be more successful in our personal and company development if we surround ourselves with people who value similar things.

Bob's Case Study

The client and coach/consultant worked together to maintain focus and momentum. The urgency of the organizational situation supported the client in continuing to focus on delivering business results. By combining the personal and organizational work with the same coach/consultant, the client was able to connect the daily work with his development. The coach was able to structure discussions to bring focus to developmental opportunities in the context of delivering business results. Given the amount of work that needed to be accomplished in a short time, the combination of coaching and consulting really worked for this client. Another key factor was that the client and coach had a high trust/high learning relationship. Had the client been less trusting or less open to learning, this process would have delivered considerably less value. The client saw significant progress in the organizational projects, while his individual change was easier to see on some days and harder on others.

During the process, the client has moved close to entering an Individualist perspective. At this stage, he is demonstrating a much higher focus on his own growth and development. He has joined a spiritual group, and he is actively involved in both educational programs and a community of people focused on not only spiritual practices but also reinforcing the belief system consistent with the values of Individualist thinking. Joining this community with his wife and maintaining work with his coach will offer the support and encouragement to maintain his transition.

In several areas, the client moved from implementing short-term tactics to reach goals to creating and using long-term practices to realize a sense of transformation in thinking and behavior. These practices supported his short-term growth, and they will continue to sustain his gains and create additional growth long term.

While his colleagues may be operating from earlier developmental views, they, too, are becoming aware of better functioning within the new environment due to the organizational changes, including restructuring the organization to align roles and responsibilities with skills and abilities. The organization has a solid infrastructure that includes vision, values, goals, results tracking, policies and procedures, and processes. All of these areas have additionally created a form of practice for the business to follow.

Bob: I had the best of both worlds. I had a business consultation from an experienced manager in combination with personal leadership coaching. As I faced new challenges and pushed forward, the lines between where one ended and the other began blurred. The solutions to complex problems involved as much who I was going to be, as they did what I was going to do.

Organizational innovation always involves bringing change through a lot of involved individuals. To discount solutions involving interpersonal dynamics, politics, perceptions, and other intangibles is gravely naïve. The functional objective might be black and white, but the success of getting there has a variety of shades. Some of these action plans were akin to typical MBA-type PowerPoint slides, and others were more like models of human behavior. The collaboration with the coach allowed me to plan through all aspects of these challenges as needed.

Carl's Case Study

Advisor: On the personal side, it is now time to revisit goals and make sure they are updated for the new year. This is happening as part of our beginning-year planning process.

On the personal side, Carl and I are back to working more on his personal development now that he has completed some major activities. He is currently focusing on improving and increasing his communication, and determining how he should invest his time going forward. We are in the process of defining how those changes are occurring now. One key element is sticking to the communication routine to ensure everyone is informed and involved. As the broader group of employees gets involved in the change, his communication role will increase.

Another area Carl is concentrating on is taking a more visible role in the community. Participating in this activity (writing a case study) is one example of this effort. This increased visibility is one example of a significant change for him, as MT leadership was not visible in the community in a leadership role. Carl's father supported the community in several concrete ways, including taking a significant role in renovating the downtown of Mansfield. The difference in actions is that Carl is stepping forward as the CEO of MT and speaking and writing to build the company image.

On the organizational side, we are still taking action, addressing barriers, and embedding innovation systematically at the end of year one. Carl decided one of the most efficient ways to move forward was to start a 12-month series of workshops. The leadership team will participate every other month to build skills and set direction. On alternating months, selected members of this team will roll out the changes to the next level of leadership. This workshop series started with performance management; we launched a class where we rolled out the new performance appraisal forms that focus on both results and behaviors rooted in the culture.

Each leader defined their objectives for the year, using the results of their MAP and 360° assessment to identify key behaviors necessary to accomplish these results, creating a development plans based on the results. This process will continue to happen annually to reinforce the increased focus on accountability and development. The senior leaders participated in the workshop with the next level leaders to reinforce the importance of this process and their expectation that both the culture and processes are changing; each leader is then expected to carry these changes back to their location. These workshops are also the time for the two groups to identify barriers to the new processes and refine the processes.

Upcoming sessions will include:

- Defining Changes and Building a Scorecard
- Coaching and Conversations for Results – Aligning Behavior with the Scorecard
- Build Change Plans Using Computer-Based Simulation
- Enhancing Strategic Thinking – Decision Making and Problem Solving
- Building Team Alignment Including Accelerating Trust Building
- Enhancing Situational Leadership
- Building Resilience – Building the Personal Qualities that Promote Personal and Team Capacity Building

While these workshops will be only a part of the process to embed systematic innovation, they are an important way to expand the change to a broader group of participants in a planned and organized manner.

Bruce's Case Study

Before I started my journey, if you had asked me about meditation, I would have shrugged it off and said that it was not important. At the same time, being a strong introvert, I practiced it, but from a more shallow perspective. Now, I find it critical to maintaining focus and ensuring that I am heading in a direction that will help me achieve my overall vision. For me, I use three key types of meditation: prayer, running, and quiet time. While part of my meditation may be simply for the sake of calming myself, most of it is actually for the purpose of cutting out the noise in my life and focusing on a few issues that I am looking to understand. If I have a particular problem that I am attempting to work through, I take time through my meditation to evaluate what has happened up to this point, evaluate my options, and determine my next steps.

I have found that by doing so through meditation, I am able to cut away more of the noise and clutter to better see and understand the issue at hand. Also, by taking time to meditate on a regular basis, I am able to better keep myself on track with my desired goals and vision. Too often, I find that there are many distractions in life, and they will readily divert me from my planned path if I do not do something to keep myself focused. The mediation also allows me time to look at my vision and values, and take time to validate them and ensure that they are what I still desire and want to work towards.

Another key step, and one that I have not been able to do the past couple of months, is having someone to talk with about my vision and goals on a regular basis, at least from a professional point of view. One of the key people I had in my support group moved on to a new job opportunity in another state, and this has left a void that I am working to fill. I find that talking with someone about my plans and what I am doing creates a level of accountability that I would not have otherwise.

A final key step that I used originally when I began my journey, and that I am starting to use again, is a journal. Again, it is a physical tool I can use to focus my thoughts and literally see what I have done, how effective my actions have been, and where I am planning to go. It provides me something that I can review on a regular basis and evaluate my progress. There is something very cathartic for me in being able to put my thoughts to paper, or, in my case, a Word document. I find that I can put my thoughts down more effectively when I am typing than I ever could when writing with pen and paper.

Your Individual Process to Embed Innovation Systematically

Now that you have explored Jill's reflections as well as the narratives of Bob, Carl, and Bruce, it is time to complete the worksheets and answer these questions for yourself. We encourage you to complete all of the exercises and answer 1-3 questions from each quadrant in the reflection question exercise.

In summary, this chapter serves to help you create an action plan and conduct thought experiments necessary to sustain the changes you have invested so much time to generate. In the current times, we culturally reinforce the idea of lifestyle changes, such as exercise and diet. Yet, this is also true of developmental growth, awareness, and skill building. To sustain the changes you have made and continue to build on them, it is important for you to continually engage them with deliberation and a sense of presence.

In our dynamic environment, growth and development are simply required just to stay relevant. This is perhaps more true now than at any other time in history, where growth is now a requirement to achieve and maintain success. Thus, realizing tangle growth is not only a matter of conceptual and pragmatic learning, but also introspecting into and engaging the relationship with ourselves and others.

CHAPTER 12:
Conclusion

Celebrate

Congratulations! You have finished the book, and we trust you have seen significant increase in your professional and personal effectiveness if you have been using the workbook over the past six months or so. It is time to celebrate your successes and the support you received from others! How will you acknowledge what you have accomplished? Consider reviewing your vision and SWOT analysis, and write down what you accomplished.

How will you acknowledge the support others provided? How, in your culture, do you show gratitude and appreciation? When will you celebrate with your support team, either individually or collectively? Have you already been celebrating?

Bob's Case Study

Bob's MAP score indicated he moved from early Achiever to late Achiever. The scorer comments included, "In general, your protocol shows signs that you have been able to develop in significant ways. Given the traits and qualities mentioned above, there is good reason to believe that growth process will continue for you naturally as you develop even greater self-awareness and move into the Individualist stage."

The assessment is a series of sentence stems where the person being assessed completes the sentences. The response to one of these items really shows progress in a poignant way. One of the stems is: When I am criticized...

In the earlier assessment, his answer indicated he rejected the input and possibly the person offering the input. In the later assessment, his answer indicated he listened with the intent to understand. This later answer is critical to illustrating his ongoing progress, as individuals limit their growth when they are unwilling to accept input or understand the perspective of the person offering it. He did not indicate he would blindly accept their recommendations, but rather he would learn what the individual needed from him and decide how to respond appropriately to the input. This one response gives significant indication that continued growth is likely and acceleration of rate of growth is also possible.

Additionally, the overall number of questions scoring at all levels moved upward to show his center of gravity shifted to a later level of capacity.

DEVELOPMENTAL LEVEL		
	1st Assessment # of answers	2nd Assessment # of answers
Opportunist	2	0
Diplomat	2	1
Expert	14	5
Achiever	12	22
Individualist	5	5
Strategist	1	3

Bob: *I'm no doubt a more resilient manager with a better ability to think in terms of strategy. I've also improved my listening skills and have not only become a better leader, but also a happier person. It is a pleasure to work with someone of my coach's caliber.*

While research from McKinsey & Company and other leading researchers indicates that approximately 50% - 75% or more change efforts fail to deliver the business results they expected, this transition delivered more than promised, and it established the foundation for ongoing success. In addition to the client's individual changes, the organization experienced some significant success in their transition, including:

- Moved from operating at a loss during the transition to operating at a significant profit that will be redirected to expand services and impact on mission-related projects

- Transitioned a critical function of the organization from out-source to in-source three months ahead of schedule

- Built several technology-based solutions to support the transition

- Built the infrastructure required to operate an organization that tripled in size with the transition

- Managed the transition with consultants, thus limiting the impact to long-term staffing cost; leveraged technology to manage costs

- Documented key business processes to minimize risk associated with staff turnover and to create a strong foundation for staff growth and development

- Implemented performance management and profit-sharing processes

- Implemented transitions with NO staff turnover or attrition

- Implemented organizational measures and board reporting to provide the board better information to allow more timely and effective governance

- Expanded service offerings by improving the current accreditation process, expanding to serve international clients, and expanding into heart-failure accreditation

- Conducted research to support better performance of medical centers using their accredited processes published in the American Journal of Cardiology

What worked?

During the initial coaching, the organizational environment seemed rather stable. As the work progressed, the organization entered into a time of significant transition. The combination of coaching and consulting that focused on business outcomes allowed the client to both generate significant business results and hone individual development targeted at business operations. If the coaching had been focused more on the client's personal development, he would not have made time for this activity, as his organization needed more attention.

From my perspective, part of the value of this experience was engaging in a coaching and consulting arrangement concurrently that involved a level of exploration of solutions and transparency of thinking and assumptions. This open discourse enabled the client to check his own thinking and expand his perspective. Additionally, it exposed him to the thinking process of the Strategist developmental level. This thinking process included an examination of assumptions, long-term impacts, involvement and perspective of multiple stakeholders, and other factors depending on the specific situation. The client remained open and receptive during the entire process. I believe this openness contributed significantly to his development. On a personal note, it also made the work a real joy for me.

The leader returned to his spiritual practice while engaging in the coaching. He had a strong foundation that had lapsed. After re-engaging in his practice, he appeared calmer and better able to deal with his daily challenges. This renewed attraction to spiritual practice will likely support his development to later developmental levels.

Bob: *The business success that I had during this period was simply phenomenal. Coming into it, it seemed like the worst of all possible scenarios, yet by the end, almost all objectives were exceeded. When I talk about what we actually did during this time, people shake their heads and ask whether I realize how remarkable it is. Oddly, the more I developed as a change leader, the less unusual I found the successes. I began to "just know" that it was going to work out. I developed a confidence, not only in myself, but also in the organization. What I really take pride in are the personal successes. People began to spontaneously volunteer to me that I "had changed." I was a better man in ways that I could see in my interactions with people every day.*

Strangely, the dazzling business results that I had in the organization were no longer all that important to me as the main definers of who I was and what I was worth. Sure, I was happy to have been a good shepherd to the organizational transition, but it wasn't the change in the organization that provided my most satisfaction; it was who I had become. It is a wonderfully satisfying thing to set your sights on improving yourself in significant ways and begin to look back and say that you had. The world that I lived in was different. I related to it differently and it treated me differently in return.

Issues of control just sort of became irrelevant. I had a longer-term perspective. As people raged and jostled around me, I found their actions interesting, but not personal. Aspects of my life that had given me joy as a young man were reinvigorated and became meaningful again. It seemed like I was more true to who I really was. That isn't to say that I didn't continue to make mistakes or that I could shrug off all challenges. I don't think that I can ever achieve a state that can't be improved on and, believe me, I have no doubt that I could stand a lot more work. I just want to make the point that my work had real results. Working with the coach so closely, so intently, for so long, did transform me in ways that I could see and others could too.

What would we change?

We are very satisfied with the client's growth and his organization's success. However, we probably focused too much on the business changes without tying them back to the overall leadership development goals more often, given the time-frames involved. We all may have missed some opportunities to explore our approaches and assumptions more deeply because of the volume of work to be delivered.

Bob: *I have no regrets. You can't contemplate your navel when the roof is caving in. I got what I needed when I needed it. Over the long haul, with the help of the coach, I was able to transform an organization and transform a man. How often do you get to do that?*

Carl's Case Study

The changes were focused on both leadership development and organizational transformation. Carl understood that he needed to enhance his skills to enable him to succeed his father in running the company and to transform the successful company to meet the needs of the next generation of clients. His personal insight led him to select a consultant and coach that used the integral approach to business transformation. Specifically, Carl understood that business and personal change must be addressed concurrently to increase the speed of the transformation.

As of this writing, the project has been going for one year. The findings are preliminary, but as of this time, we are seeing strong indicators of success that include:

- Defined organization mission and vision
- Defined organizational guiding principles as the foundation for the culture
- Defined a scorecard to track results aligned with the vision, mission, and guiding principles

- Reduced the number of employees in 3 key functions based on industry benchmarks to maintain profitability during a down economy

- Assessed key leaders, and began a coaching and development program

- Successful launch of a wholly owned subsidiary to respond to the needs of the technology market. Separating the businesses will allow the leadership of the core business to focus on delivering results to current clients, while the new business is able to focus on a very different life-cycle phase of launching a new company.

- Successful reorganization of leadership roles in conjunction with the new business launch

- Improving all key organizational functions to support the increased business complexity

- Launched a Project Management Office (PMO) to oversee the large volume of projects to ensure all investments in projects are aligned with the strategy and effectively use resources

- Launched new performance management system to set goals and reward accomplishments aligned with the vision, mission, and guiding principles

- Defined and launched a 12- month leadership development and organizational transformation program that will build additional skills, reinforce culture changes, and develop leaders deeper in the organization

- Buy-in from key leaders in support of significant changes and support for the overall direction of the company going forward

This has been a very challenging year. While the results are good, getting here was a challenging process that required strong resolve and courage. I mentioned earlier in the article that everyone acted with commitment to the company and with a high level of integrity. This commitment to doing the right thing made a huge impact on the overall success. Many people would have given up when faced with the difficulties of this process. I have a deep appreciation for all of the members of the leadership team, and I feel quite honored to be involved in this process. I believe I have learned a great deal from them, and I continue this project into year two as a better person.

Carl: *We accomplished a tremendous amount of improvement this year, not only in doing things differently but also by thinking differently as a group. At times, the process seemed slow, but in retrospect; it was impressive as to the amount of ground we covered. We are very fortunate that we have a management team that wants the best for the company. As they began to see what we were doing for the company, the buy-in and participation increased. While it is never perfect, it is certainly much better than it was last year.*

This is what I can report after my twelfth month in the process:

- *First, there is a clearly articulated and written plan; we are all marching in the same relative direction. No longer do we have seven lone wolves running their locations with no unified course of action, other than to sell and service more.*

- *Second, we are addressing the sacred cows (people and processes) that have held us hostage for many years; they are being identified and eliminated. Because of this, our expenses are dropping while productivity is increasing - imagine that!*

- *Third, our decisions are more aligned with data and industry benchmarks rather than intuition or politics. Now if a project is dying, we know sooner and we either increase the resources or pull the plug. It no longer hovers in project limbo.*

- *Fourth, there is better utilization of resources due to organizational changes and the establishment of a Project Management Office. Roles are better clarified.*

- *Fifth, there is less drama. While this seems minor at first blush, it is huge. We are now focused on the issues rather than the personalities. Keep in mind we have a great work environment and everyone gets along very well. But the mild undertow of drama from unclear objectives sucked valuable energy out of everyone.*

These are just five results out of many which we have experienced, but it should give you a small sense of what is possible. For the next twelve months, I am focusing on improving the processes, and I will be spending considerable time developing our team. I am also pleased to report that after eleven months of resistance, these same senior leaders are now seeking out the Advisor to discuss issues rather than ducking down the hall when they see her coming their way. Maybe they are catching on.

What worked?

Advisor: This experience has reinforced for me how critical an integral approach is to organizational transformation. Carl is a strong leader who wanted to make significant changes to his organization. I think this process was significantly more effective because he started with his own personal changes then moved to organizational change.

In this case, having an outside consultant who was not part of the family or the organization was of benefit. I have no interest other than my client's success. I gained some level of credibility because of my experience doing this type of transition, as well as a strong set of tools. I also tried to remain impartial during the process.

Carl invested as much as 20% of his time in working with me. This significant commitment accelerated the process significantly. The investment allowed him to both develop his personal leadership skills and plan the desired change. Beyond the time we spent together, he spent a great deal of office and personal time implementing the changes. His unwavering commitment to transforming himself and MT kept us on track and allowed us to maintain momentum and credibility. While at times it seemed we were not moving, in retrospect, we made significant changes in a very short time without major disruption to the company. Additionally, all of the senior leaders remain with the company as of this writing.

The commitment of the senior leaders to the company was nothing short of amazing. There were times of significant frustration and difference of perspective. These men chose to stick together and work through the differences, putting the company before their egos and self-interest. Because of this, they remain intact and stronger than before. While I cannot speak for what they experienced, I can say with certainty that I have very high regard for every one of them for what they have accomplished; who they were as people and the integrity they demonstrated during the challenging times.

Carl: Part of our culture involved the mindset that each location was autonomous and each manager did what he wanted. Our belief was that we wanted each General Manager to be an entrepreneur. While this belief still holds true today, we now have a unified vision and mission, and standardized processes. Process standardization was probably one of the hardest culture changes we encountered.

What would we change?

Advisor: I did not emphasize communication with the broader organization enough. Because of what I perceived as a lack of shared vision, I focused on working with the leaders I thought were on board and interested in moving forward. I think I would have tried harder to build bridges and build support with key stakeholders if I could have reconciled the differences more quickly. While in the end the result has been positive, I wonder if more communication earlier in the process might have reduced the organizational stress.

Carl: One of my challenges has been to provide meaningful communication. Some managers wanted to be involved daily, while others prefer month-to-month meetings. I have now taken the path of over communication, and I occasionally receive complaints today that we have too many meetings, but interestingly enough, no complaints that they would rather be a bit more in the dark. Moving forward, we will be able to reduce the number of meetings as we become more organized by using tools like the Scorecard and Project Management Office.

What Is Next For You?

Through this book, we provided a framework for innovative leadership and a process to support your development. We augmented the process with a series of practical questions and templates that can serve as guides. Based on our work with several hundred clients over the last five years, we offer this specific combination of tools and frameworks to create a comprehensive framework and practical tools that will allow you, the leader, to define what you want to change and also have a road map that will support your development.

Additionally, we provided the story of Jill to illustrate how to use the development process. She uses the tools in the book and answers the questions to illustrate how a strategist level leader would engage in development. It is through Jill's explorations that we share the practical application of this theory with you.

Now that you have completed the Field Book for the first round and you have established a solid personal development practice, it is time to think about whether you want to enhance your practice and begin the process again. Do you want to build on what you have created and revisit parts of the Field Book that may be valuable at this time? You could start from the beginning and confirm your vision and values. The future iterations will likely take less time as you are have experience with the development process. You may find that you focus in different areas based on your growth. As you noticed in the description of levels, each developmental level will place its focus on different elements during the process.

As a reminder, for a person actively working on your development, moving up a developmental level may take between 2-6 years per level. You have a great start, now celebrate and reaffirm your commitment to your own growth!

Resources

This section includes additional recommendations to augment the fieldbook for those who want more in-depth information.

Resources Chapter 2

The theoretical research of Susann Cook-Greuter and Terri O'Fallon provide the most recent and complete references available in support of Developmental levels and their applications. Both can be found on their websites.

www.cook-greuter.com
www.pacificintegral.com

Resources Chapter 5

For more information about The Leadership Circle Profile - see the study written by Bob Anderson and published by *The Leadership Circle, The Leadership Circle and Organizational Performance, 2007.*

www.theleadershipcircle.com

Resources Chapter 6

Book: Parker Palmer, *Let Your Life Speak – Listen for the Voice of Vocation.* San Francisco: Jossey Bass, 2000.

Resources Chapter 7

- Mature Adult Profile Assessment (MAP) www.pacificintegral.com
- The Leadership Circle 360 Assessment www.theleadershipcircle.com
- Resilience Assessment www.metcalf-associates.com
- Enneagram www.enneagraminstitute.com

Resources Chapter 8

- Book: Robert Fritz. "Tool: Structural Tension," *Path of Least Resistance, Learning to Become the Creative Force in Your Own Life.* New York: Random House, 1989.

- Book: Bill Torbert and Associates. *Action Inquiry, The Secret of Timely and Transforming Leadership.* San Francisco: Jossey-Bass, 2004.

- Book: Kerry Patterson, Joseph Grenny, Ron McMillan, Al Switzler. *Crucial Conversations: Tools for Talking when Stakes are High.* San Francisco: McGraw-Hill, 2002.

- Book: Art Kleiner, Peter Senge, Richard Ross, Bryan Smith, Charlotte Roberts. *Fifth Discipline Fieldbook, Strategies and Tools for Building a Learning Organization.* New York: Crown Business Books, 1994.

- Book: George Leonard and Michael Murphy. *The Life We Are Given, A Long Term Program for Realizing Potential of Body, Mind, Heart and Soul.* New York: Tarcher/Putnam, 1995.

- DVDs: Integral Life Practice Starter Kit. Integral Institute (3-2-1 shadow workshop and Big Mind).

- Online resource and tools: Heartmath meditation practices and emWave to monitor heart activity. www.heartmath.org.

Resources Chapter 9

Book: Art Kleiner, Peter Senge, Richard Ross, Bryan Smith, Charlotte Roberts. "Conversational Recipes," *Fifth Discipline Fieldbook, Strategies and Tools for Building a Learning Organization.* New York: Crown Business Books, 1994.

Book: Kerry Patterson, Joseph Grenny, Ron McMillan, Al Switzler. *Crucial Conversations: Tools for Talking when Stakes are High.* San Francisco: McGraw-Hill, 2002.

Resources Chapter 10

Book: Bill Torbert and Associates. *Action Inquiry, The Secret of Timely and Transforming Leadership.^* San Francisco: Jossey-Bass, 2004.

Book: Robert Kegan and Lisa Laskow Lahey. *How the Way We Talk can Change the Way We Work.* Boston: Harvard Business School Publishing, 2009.

DVD: Shadow Module 3-2-1 Process with Diane Hamilton; Integral Life Practice Series produced by Integral Institute.

References

Barrett Brown. Conscious Leadership for Sustainability: How Leaders with Late-Stage Action Logic Design and Engage in Sustainability Initiatives. Doctoral Dissertation, Fielding Graduate University. 2011.

Jim Collins. *Good to Great: Why some Companies Make the Leap… and Others Don't.* New York: HarperCollins Publishers, Inc., 2001.

Susanne Cook-Greuter. *"A Detailed Description of Nine Action Logics in the Leadership Development Framework Adapted from Leadership Development Theory,"* www.cook-greuter.com. 2002.

Mihaly Csikszentihalyi, Flow: *The Psychology of Optimal Experience.* New York: Harper Perennial, 1990.

Geoff Fitch, Venita Ramirez, and Terri O'Fallon. "Enacting Containers for Integral Transformative Development." Presented July 2010 Integral Theory Conference.

Alain Gauthier, "Developing Generative Change Leaders Across Sectors: An Exploration of Integral Approaches", *Integral Leadership Review,* June 2008.

Daniel Goleman, *Working with Emotional Intelligence.* New York: Bantam Books, 1998

Daniel Goleman, Richard E. Boyatzis and Annie McKee, *Primal Leadership: Learning to Lead with Emotional Intelligence.* Boston: Harvard Business School Press, 2002.

Daniel Goleman, *Emotional Intelligence.* New York: Bantam Books, 1995.

Roxanne Howe-Murphy, Roxanne, Don Richard Riso, and Russ Hudson. *Deep Coaching: Using the Enneagram as a Catalyst for Profound Change,* El Granada: Enneagram Press, 2007.

Maryanna Klatt, Janet Buckworth, and William B. Malarkey. "Effects of Low-Dose Mindfulness-Based Stress Reduction (MBSR-ld) on Working Adults." Health Education and Behavior. Vol. 36, no. 3. 2009: 601-614.

Salvatore R. Maddi and Deborah M. Khoshaba, *Resilience at Work: How to Succeed No Matter What Life Throws at You.* New York: MJF Books, 2005.

Maureen Metcalf. "Level 5 Leadership: Leadership that Transforms Organizations and Creates Sustainable Results." *Integral Leadership Review.* March 2008.

Maureen Metcalf, John Forman, and Dena Paluck. "Implementing Sustainable Transformation – Theory and Application." *Integral Leadership Review.* June 2008.

Maureen Metcalf and Dena Paluck. "The Story of Jill—How an Individual Leader Developed into a "Level 5" Leader." *Integral Leadership Review.* June 2010

Peter G. Northhouse. *Leadership: Theory and Practice.* Thousand Oaks: Sage Publications, 2010.

Terri O'Fallon, Venita Ramirez, Jesse McKay, Kari Mays. "Collective Individualism: Experiments in Second Tier Community." Presented August, 2008 at the Integral Theory Conference

Terri O'Fallon. "The Collapse of the Wilber-Combs Matrix: The Interpenetration of the State and Structure Stages." Presented July, 2010 at the Integral Theory Conference (1st place winner)

Terri O'Fallon. "Integral Leadership Development: Overview of our Leadership Development Approach." www.pacificintegral.com, 2011.

Hilke R. Richmer. An Analysis of the Effects Of Enneagram-Based Leader Development On Self-Awareness: A Case Study At A Midwest Utility Company Doctoral Dissertation, Spalding University. 2011.

Don Richard Riso, and Russ Hudson. *The Wisdom of the Enneagram: The Complete Guide to Psychological and Spiritual Growth for the Nine Personality Types.* New York: Bantam, 1999.

Don Richard Riso and Russ Hudson. *Personality Types: Using the Enneagram for Self-Discovery.* New York: Houghton Mifflin, 1996.

David Rooke and William R. Torbert, "Seven Transformations of Leadership, Leaders are made, not born, and how they develop is critical for organizational change", *Harvard Business Review,* April 2005.

David Rooke and William R. Torbert. "Organizational Transformation as a Function of CEOs' Developmental Stage." Organization Development Journal 16, 1, 1998: 11-28.

Bill Torbert and Associates. *Action Inquiry – The Secret of Timely and Transforming Leadership.* San Francisco: Berrett-Koehler Publishing, Inc. 2004.

Peter Senge, Art Kleiner, Charlotte Roberts, Richard Ross, and Bryan Smith. *The Fifth Discipline Fieldbook: Strategies and Tools for Building a Learning Organization.* New York: Doubleday, 1994.

Cindy Wigglesworth, "Why Spiritual Intelligence Is Essential to Mature Leadership", *Integral Leadership Review* August, 2006.

Ken Wilber. "Introduction to Integral Theory and Practice: IOS Basic and AQAL Map." www.integralnaked.org. 2003.

About the Authors

Maureen Metcalf

Maureen Metcalf is the Founder and CEO of Metcalf & Associates, Inc. a management consulting and coaching firm dedicated to helping leaders, their management teams and organizations implement the innovative leadership practices necessary to thrive in a rapidly changing environment.

Maureen is an acclaimed thought leader who developed, tested, and implemented emerging models that dramatically improve leaders and organizations success in changing times. She works with leaders to develop innovative leadership capacity and with organizations to further develop innovative leadership qualities. Maureen is on the forefront of helping organizations to explore these emerging solutions for long term organizational sustainability.

As a Senior Manager with two "Big Four" Management consulting firms for 12 years, Maureen managed and contributed to the successful completion of a wide array of projects from strategy development and organizational design for start-up companies to large system change for well-established organizations. She has worked with a number of Fortune 100 clients delivering a wide range of significant business results such as: increased profitability, cycle time reduction, increased employee engagement and effectiveness, and improved quality.

Mark Palmer

Mark Palmer is a Principal with Metcalf & Associates, Inc., a professional services firm specializing in leadership development, team building, and organizational effectiveness. Mark is a founding member of the Integral Institute, an international think-tank created to combine progressive academic research with practical applications in the public and private sector. He is an accomplished teacher, has conducted numerous seminars and lectured extensively on business leadership supported by social theory. Mark has also taught several online courses and served as the institute's Program Director for Integral Practice.

Mark Palmer is a writer, editor and full-time professional specializing in Organization and Social Science research; he is also a pioneering expert in the design and application of Innovative Leadership. His background includes Economics, Social and Behavioral Theory, Cultural Studies, and Anthropology.

Mark is an expert on the theoretical work of American born philosopher Ken Wilber, and has written extensively, for private circulation, on the application of Wilber's work to numerous disciplines. He was the senior editor of The Simple Feeling of Being, published in 2004 as a compilation of Wilber's work spanning 25 years.

Mark is also the head of Store Development Research and GIS Services for Wendy's International, Inc., providing strategic planning to support senior and executive management.

CPSIA information can be obtained at www.ICGtesting.com
Printed in the USA
BVOW061157071212

307544BV00004B/43/P